T0215382

SQL Server on Kubernetes

Designing and Building a Modern Data Platform

Anthony E. Nocentino
Ben Weissman

Foreword by Bob Ward

Apress®

SQL Server on Kubernetes: Designing and Building a Modern Data Platform

Anthony E. Nocentino
Oxford, MS, USA

Ben Weissman
Nürnberg, Bayern, Germany

ISBN-13 (pbk): 978-1-4842-7191-9
https://doi.org/10.1007/978-1-4842-7192-6

ISBN-13 (electronic): 978-1-4842-7192-6

Managing Director, Apress Media LLC: Welmoed Spahr
Acquisitions Editor: Jonathan Gennick
Development Editor: Laura Berendson
Coordinating Editor: Jill Balzano

Cover image designed by Freepik (www.freepik.com)

Distributed to the book trade worldwide by Springer Science+Business Media LLC, 1 New York Plaza, Suite 4600, New York, NY 10004. Phone 1-800-SPRINGER, fax (201) 348-4505, e-mail orders-ny@springer-sbm.com, or visit www.springeronline.com. Apress Media, LLC is a California LLC and the sole member (owner) is Springer Science + Business Media Finance Inc (SSBM Finance Inc). SSBM Finance Inc is a **Delaware** corporation.

For information on translations, please e-mail booktranslations@springernature.com; for reprint, paperback, or audio rights, please e-mail bookpermissions@springernature.com.

Apress titles may be purchased in bulk for academic, corporate, or promotional use. eBook versions and licenses are also available for most titles. For more information, reference our Print and eBook Bulk Sales web page at http://www.apress.com/bulk-sales.

Any source code or other supplementary material referenced by the author in this book is available to readers on GitHub via the book's product page, located at www.apress.com/9781484271919. For more detailed information, please visit http://www.apress.com/source-code.

Printed on acid-free paper

To my girls. I love you.
—Anthony

For Gwendolyn and Franzie.
—Ben

Table of Contents

About the Authors

Anthony E. Nocentino is the founder and president of Centino Systems as well as a Pluralsight author, a Microsoft Data Platform MVP, and an industry-recognized Kubernetes, SQL Server, and Linux expert. In his consulting practice, Anthony designs solutions, deploys the technology, and provides expertise on system performance, architecture, and security. He has bachelor's and master's degrees in computer science, with research publications in machine virtualization, high-performance/low-latency data access algorithms, and spatial database systems.

Ben Weissman is the owner and founder of Solisyon, a consulting firm based in Germany and focused on business intelligence (BI), business analytics, and data warehousing. He is a Microsoft Data Platform MVP and the first German BimlHero and has been working with SQL Server since SQL Server 6.5. Ben is also an MCSE and Charter Member of the Microsoft Professional Program for Big Data, Artificial Intelligence, and Data Science, and he is a Certified Data Vault Data Modeler. He has published multiple books and video courses and is a regular speaker at international events. If he is not currently working with data, he is probably traveling to explore the world. You can find him online at @bweissman on Twitter.

About the Technical Reviewer

**Andrew Pruski** is a SQL Server DBA, Microsoft Data Platform MVP, and Certified Kubernetes Administrator. Originally from Swansea, Wales, he is now based in Dublin, Ireland.

Andrew has spent the last few years delving into the container platform, has written multiple articles about running SQL Server in containers, and has spoken at multiple events across Europe and America.

You can find him blogging at *dbafromthecold.com*.

Acknowledgments

First and foremost, I need to thank my wife, Heather. You are my best friend and partner. This year we celebrate 21 years of marriage together. Every single day with you is better than the previous one. I love you and thank you for all of your unwavering support, inspiration over the years, and listening to me ramble on about tech stuff. I want to thank my two loving daughters, Gabby and Charlotte, for "SQL Server, SQL Server, SQL Server...," "Kubernetes is a fancy drink," and "Sassy Sausage." I love you, girls. You are an endless source of joy and pride to me.

Next, thank you to the SQL and Data Platform MVP communities. So many of you have contributed to who I am today as a person and technologist. I want to call out my coauthor, Ben Weissman, for your friendship and helping me push this book forward – thank you. I want to also say thanks to my container-mate Andrew Pruski, who is originally from Wales but now based in Dublin. Andrew and I are constantly talking about all things SQL Server, containers, and Kubernetes. Thank you for reviewing this book.

To the many friends on the SQL Server Engineering Team that I have made over the last few years, thank you for your endless technical innovations, engagement in the SQL Server community, and replying to my emails. You put SQL Server on Linux, then in containers, and then on Kubernetes...an amazing feat.

To Bob Ward, thank you for writing an amazing foreword, for being such an enormous part of the SQL Server community, and for teaching the world how SQL Server works under the hood.

To the Apress team, Jonathan, Jill, and Laura, you've truly made this process easy. We couldn't have done this without your support.

—Anthony

ACKNOWLEDGMENTS

Thank you, Franzie! For the last 11 years (and the next!). For supporting me in everything I do. And for our beautiful daughter. I love you both – the mostesterest.

Thank you, Solisyon team! For delivering excellence every single day – even in challenging times like these!

Thank you, #sqlsaturdaycambridge! This is where Anthony and I met back in the day.

Thank you, Anthony! This was another fun project – what are we going to do next? While we figure this out, thank you for being who you are, and thank you for being a great friend!

Thank you, #sqlfamily. I may have said this before: I have never seen a community like ours, and it's an honor to be part of it. There are way too many to call you all out – but you know who you are.

Thank you, Andrew! For regular fun conversations on Twitter, for helping out whenever I bother you with anything, and for being an amazing tech reviewer for this book!

And last but not least, thank you, Bob – for your support with this book and, even more, everything you do for our community!

—Ben

Foreword

SQL Server has been a force in the database industry for developers, enterprises, and small businesses for decades. For years, Windows Server was the prominent platform where SQL Server cut its teeth. In 2017, we launched the ability to run SQL Server on Linux operating systems, which was a game changer for us and for the database community.

SQL Server's support for Linux opens up our community to the wonderful technology of containers. Containers unlock new possibilities for portability, flexibility, efficiency, and optimization. SQL Server is now part of that world and ecosystem. With the support for containers comes the natural extension of Kubernetes, a system to deploy and manage containerized applications like SQL Server at scale.

This book, written by two experts in the industry, Anthony Nocentino and Ben Weissman, is your best source to learn about SQL Server and Kubernetes. I have personally worked with both Anthony and Ben, and I can't think of more capable authors for this subject.

I love the way this book is organized for the reader. You will build your knowledge by starting with the fundamentals of containers, the Kubernetes architecture, and the details of deploying k8s. (Yes, you need to learn to call it that. Who wants to type the full name every time?) Armed with the knowledge of k8s fundamentals such as how to use the famous kubectl tool and storage concepts, you will learn all aspects of deploying, interacting with, and monitoring SQL Server on k8s. Along your journey with each chapter are many step-by-step examples and figures so you can visually confirm your experiences with SQL and k8s.

The book concludes with great examples of SQL Server containers on k8s in real-world production scenarios including Azure Arc and SQL Server Big Data Clusters (BDC). SQL Server is everywhere you need it, and learning how SQL Server containers run on k8s is all about innovation with new platforms, new challenges, and new skills. This book will help you meet those challenges written by two of the experts in the SQL Server and platform industry and community.

—Bob Ward
Microsoft

PART I

Container and Kubernetes Foundations

CHAPTER 1

Getting Started

Welcome to *SQL Server on Kubernetes*! This chapter introduces the lab architecture and technical requirements that you'll need to have in place to perform the labs in this book. The first set of labs is based on deploying SQL Server in a container on a Docker host. Then we'll progress to deploying SQL Server and other applications into a Kubernetes cluster that we will help you build later in the book.

Installing Docker

In Chapter 2, we will introduce containers and deploying SQL Server as a container. To perform the labs in that chapter, you will need an installation of Docker on a computer and the `sqlcmd` utility. If you prefer using another command line–based SQL client like `mssql-cli`, that is fine too. However, for simplicity, we will stick to `sqlcmd` in our demos.

Docker is available for Windows, MacOS, and Linux platforms, each of which has a unique installation method. While you can install Docker on any of these platforms and the Chapter 2 demos will work, we're going to suggest for this course to create a virtual machine (VM) with two vCPUs, 8GB of RAM and 150GB of disk space, and install Ubuntu 18.04 as the base operating system.

Here are links to the installation instructions for Docker on its various platforms. Please review the installation requirements for installing Docker on each of these platforms. If you want to replicate the demos in Chapter 2, you will need to have this environment in place first:

- **Docker Desktop for Windows:** *https://docs.docker.com/docker-for-windows/install/*

- **Docker Desktop for Mac:** *https://docs.docker.com/docker-for-mac/install/*

- **Docker Engine – Community (Ubuntu):** *https://docs.docker.com/install/linux/docker-ce/ubuntu/*

© Anthony E. Nocentino, Ben Weissman 2021
A. E. Nocentino and B. Weissman, *SQL Server on Kubernetes*, https://doi.org/10.1007/978-1-4842-7192-6_1

Prior to moving on, please ensure you can successfully run a container in your environment. Execute Listing 1-1 at the command line.

Listing 1-1. Running your first Docker container

```
docker run hello-world
```

If the container runs successfully, you will see the output shown in Listing 1-2.

Listing 1-2. Output of your first Docker container

```
Unable to find image 'hello-world:latest' locally
latest: Pulling from library/hello-world
1b930d010525: Pull complete
Digest: sha256:9572f7cdcee8591948c2963463447a53466950b3fc15a247fcad1917ca215a2f
Status: Downloaded newer image for hello-world:latest

Hello from Docker!
This message shows that your installation appears to be working correctly.

To generate this message, Docker took the following steps:
 1. The Docker client contacted the Docker daemon.
 2. The Docker daemon pulled the "hello-world" image from the Docker Hub.
    (amd64)
 3. The Docker daemon created a new container from that image which runs the
    executable that produces the output you are currently reading.
 4. The Docker daemon streamed that output to the Docker client, which
    sent it to your terminal.

To try something more ambitious, you can run an Ubuntu container with:
 $ docker run -it ubuntu bash

Share images, automate workflows, and more with a free Docker ID:
 https://hub.docker.com/

For more examples and ideas, visit:
 https://docs.docker.com/get-started/
```

In addition to Docker, the Chapter 2 demos require the `sqlcmd` utility. You can download it from the following location:

- **SQL Server Command Line Utilities:** *https://docs.microsoft. com/en-us/sql/tools/sqlcmd-utility*

Virtual Machine–Based Kubernetes Cluster Requirements

As we move on to the Kubernetes chapters of the book, we will build a Kubernetes Cluster together in Chapter 4. To do this, we will need some compute and storage resources. For our lab, we are going to use a set of five Linux virtual machines. Each VM in our lab will need two vCPUs, 2GB of RAM and 150GB of disk space, running Ubuntu Server 16.04+ as the operating system. We have tested the code in this book on both Ubuntu 16.04 and Ubuntu 18.04. Kubernetes is supported on several operating systems. Check out *https://kubernetes.io/docs/ setup/production-environment/tools/ kubeadm/install-kubeadm/* for more details.

Running Virtual Machines in Azure

If you don't have a system that supports running these virtual machines, another option is to set them up in Azure. We have provided you a script that will set up the entire environment for you. This will require an active Azure subscription as well as the *Azure CLI (command line interface)*. You can download the *Azure CLI* from *https://docs. microsoft.com/en-us/cli/azure/*, and we will also show you an easy way of installing it from the command line in the section "Install Tools." If you do not have an Azure subscription, you can sign up for a trial account at *https://azure.microsoft.com/ en-us/free/*. This will give you a $200 credit for 30 days to use any Azure service.

Before we can interact with Azure through the Azure CLI, we need to log in, which happens through the command shown in Listing 1-3.

Listing 1-3. Login script to your Azure account using the Azure CLI

```
az login
```

This will open a web browser on Windows and a Mac or point you to a URL on Linux to confirm your credentials.

If you have access to multiple Azure subscriptions, make sure you are using the right one by using the command in Listing 1-4. Should you be prompted to install any extensions for the Azure CLI, please do so.

Listing 1-4. Set the Azure CLI's active subscription

```
az account set -s <YourSubscription>
```

Now you can run the script in Listing 1-5, which will create a resource group, a virtual network, network security rules that allow inbound RDP and SSH connections from ANY IP address, and the virtual machines as described in the previous section. This will also generate public DNS entries, which by their nature must be unique, so please modify the following variables in the script based on your requirements:

- Username
- PW (the password to be used)
- Region (the Azure region where all resources will be created)
- dnsPrefix (prefix being added to all public DNS names)
- RG (resource group name)

Note   It is not advisable to have your machines being reachable from any public IP address, so do not use any sensitive data in this lab environment. The *dnsPrefix* must be globally unique, so change this to something containing your initials and/ or random numbers.

Listing 1-5. PowerShell script to create a lab environment using Azure VMs

```
# Modify these variables as needed
$Region="EastUS"
$RG="KubernetesLabs"
$Username="labuser"
$PW="Str@ngPassw0rd"
$dnsPrefix="k8slab"
```

```
$VMSize="Standard_B2s"
$Linux_Image="Canonical:UbuntuServer:18.04-LTS:latest"
$Windows_Image="Win2016datacenter"

#Define machines
$machines = ConvertFrom-Csv @'
Hostname,IP,OS
storage,172.16.94.5,Linux
control,172.16.94.10,Linux
node1,172.16.94.11,Linux
node2,172.16.94.12,Linux
node3,172.16.94.13,Linux
workstation,172.16.94.100,Windows
'@

# Create RG
az group create -l $Region -n $RG

# Create VNET and NSG
az network vnet create --name LABVnet --resource-group $RG --address-
prefixes 172.16.94.0/24

az network vnet subnet create --name LabSubnet --address-prefixes
172.16.94.0/24 `
    --resource-group $RG --vnet-name LABVnet

az network nsg create --name LABNSG --resource-group $RG

az network nsg rule create --name SSH --nsg-name LABNSG --priority 1000 `
    --resource-group $RG --destination-port-ranges 22 --access "Allow" `
    --protocol TCP --direction Inbound

az network nsg rule create --name RDP --nsg-name LABNSG --priority 1001 `
    --resource-group $RG --destination-port-ranges 3389 --access "Allow" `
    --protocol TCP --direction Inbound

#Create VMs
foreach($vm in $machines) {
$hostname=$vm.Hostname
```

```
$DNSName="$dnsPrefix-$hostname"
$image=$Windows_Image
if ($vm.OS -eq "Linux") { $image=$Linux_Image }
az network public-ip create --name PIP-$hostname --resource-group $RG
--dns-name $DNSName

az network nic create --name NIC-$hostname --resource-group $RG --subnet
LabSubnet `
    --vnet-name LABVnet --private-ip-address $vm.IP --public-ip-address
    PIP-$hostname

az vm create --name $hostname --resource-group $RG --nics NIC-$hostname
--os-disk-size-gb 150 `
    --os-disk-name Disk-$hostname --image $image --authentication-type
    password `
    --admin-username $Username --admin-password $PW --size $VMSize
}
```

In addition to the Linux VMs, this script has also created a Windows VM, which can be used as your administrative workstation as described later in this chapter.

Note   Make sure to delete or stop and deallocate all these resources when you don't need them anymore to avoid them generating any unnecessary cost.

Virtual Machine Network Configuration

Configure the lab VMs' IP addresses as specified in Table 1-1. You are free to use different IP addresses in your lab, but you will need to account for that in several of the labs when building your cluster. If you've opted for the Azure VM approach in the previous section, those machines will already be set up this way.

Table 1-1. *Virtual Machine Configuration*

Name	IP Address	Function
control	172.16.94.10	Control Plane Node
node1	172.16.94.11	Worker Node
node2	172.16.94.12	Worker Node
node3	172.16.94.13	Worker Node
storage	172.16.94.5	NFS Storage Server
workstation (optional)	172.16.94.100	Administrative workstation (Windows)

Next, in IT there's a saying, it's always DNS. So, for our lab, we are going to add host entries to the /etc/hosts file on each of these systems to ensure we are able to address all of the systems by name in our lab. In Listing 1-6, you will find the contents of our /etc/hosts file. Your hosts file may have entries for localhost and possibly other configurations.

Listing 1-6. Required additional Linux hosts file contents

```
172.16.94.5     storage
172.16.94.10    control
172.16.94.11    node1
172.16.94.12    node2
172.16.94.13    node3
```

If you do not know how to manually edit a file on a Linux system, you can run the script in Listing 1-7 on each of the Linux nodes.

Listing 1-7. Script to add entries to the Linux hosts file

```
echo 172.16.94.5 storage > tmphosts
echo 172.16.94.10 control >> tmphosts
echo 172.16.94.11 node1 >> tmphosts
echo 172.16.94.12 node2 >> tmphosts
echo 172.16.94.13 node3 >> tmphosts
sudo -- sh -c "cat tmphosts >> /etc/hosts"
```

On a Windows machine, you will find the file under *C:\Windows\System32\ drivers\ etc\hosts.*

Note   To edit the hosts file on Windows, make sure to run your editor as administrator.

Before moving on, please be sure that you have console or SSH access (by using the hostname) to all of these virtual machines and that they are able to connect to each other over your network.

Azure Kubernetes Service

The majority of our demos will be from our local virtual machine–based Kubernetes Cluster, but due to the cloud native-ness of Kubernetes, there are some labs in this book that will require the services of an Azure Kubernetes Service (AKS) cluster so we can highlight certain Kubernetes functionality. This will also require an Azure subscription. We will build an AKS cluster together in Chapter 4.

If you prefer to use another managed Kubernetes offering like Amazon EKS, that is fine too. However, again for reasons of simplicity, we will stick to this one example.

Install Tools

In addition to the Cluster, where we are going to deploy our demo applications and SQL Server, we will need some tools to work with the applications and databases we deploy. You can install these tools on an administrative workstation and access the applications and databases over the network. If so, you'll want to ensure that you have the /etc/hosts file entries that we specified on the cluster nodes. For lab purposes, you may consider installing these on the Control Plane Node. For production systems, this is not advisable.

We will need

- Basic tools (curl, grep, wget, SSH client)
- Kubectl
- Azure CLI

- Azdata

- SQL Server Command Line Utilities, which provides *sqlcmd – https://docs.microsoft.com/en-us/sql/tools/sqlcmd-utility*

Using a Linux Machine as Your Administrative Workstation

If you prefer to use one of your Linux machines as your administrative workstation, we need to make the Microsoft repository a trusted source using the code in Listing 1-8 and also to add the Microsoft repository to the list of known sources for package installations.

Listing 1-8. apt script for basic prerequisites

```
sudo apt-get update
sudo apt-get install gnupg ca-certificates curl wget software-properties-
common apt-transport-https lsb-release -y
curl -sL https://packages.microsoft.com/keys/microsoft.asc |
gpg --dearmor |
sudo tee /etc/apt/trusted.gpg.d/microsoft.asc.gpg > /dev/null
curl https://packages.microsoft.com/keys/microsoft.asc | sudo apt-key add -
sudo add-apt-repository "$(wget -qO- https://packages.microsoft.com/config/
ubuntu/18.04/prod.list)"
sudo apt-get update
```

Now we're ready to go ahead and install azdata, the Azure command line interface, and *kubectl* using the code from Listing 1-9.

Listing 1-9. apt script for azdata, azure-cli, sqlcmd, and kubectl

```
sudo apt-get install -y azdata-cli
sudo apt-get install -y azure-cli
sudo apt-get install -y kubectl
sudo apt-get install -y mssql-tools
```

That's it – your Ubuntu machine is ready to go for the upcoming labs.

Using a Windows Machine as Your Administrative Workstation

Many of us are Windows users and therefore prefer deploying from a Windows client. While some of the tasks in the labs must be run within the Linux environment, many can also be executed from a Windows client.

If you have opted to run your VMs in Azure, it is advisable to also have your administrative workstation there, so it sits on the same virtual network for seamless access to the Linux machines. We have created a Windows VM named *workstation* for that purpose earlier.

A Little Helper for Windows Users: Chocolatey

If you prefer using a Windows client as your administrative workstation, we also recommend using a package manager, to automate your installation.

We'd like to point your attention to Chocolatey or "choco." In case you haven't heard about it, choco is a free package manager for Windows that will allow us to install many of our prerequisites with a single line in PowerShell or a command prompt. Given that Windows Servers do not come with an easy-to-use built-in package manager, it just makes life much easier. You can find more information on *http://chocolatey.org*, and you can even create an account and provide your own packages there.

From a simple user perspective though, there is no need to create an account or to download any installer.

To make choco available on your system, open a PowerShell window in Administrative mode and run the script shown in Listing 1-10.

Listing 1-10. Install script for Chocolatey in PowerShell

```
[Net.ServicePointManager]::SecurityProtocol = [Net.ServicePointManager]::
SecurityProtocol -bor [Net.SecurityProtocolType]::Tls12
Set-ExecutionPolicy Bypass -Scope Process -Force; iex ((New-Object System.
Net.WebClient).DownloadString('https://chocolatey.org/install.ps1'))
```

Once the respective command has completed, choco is installed and ready to be used.

Tools on Windows

Now that we have a workstation and choco installed on it, let us start with a few little helpers that come with Linux by default, but are either missing or limited on Windows by default. By running the code in Listing 1-11, we'll install *curl* (to interact with websites), *grep* (to filter output on the command line), and *putty* (which also comes with *pscp*, a tool that will allow us to copy data from a Linux machine and will also act as our SSH client).

We will also be installing Chrome, as Internet Explorer (which comes with Windows Server by default) is not supported by some of the dashboards we'll be using.

Listing 1-11. Install script for recommended tools

```
choco install curl -y
choco install grep -y
choco install putty -y
choco install googlechrome -y
```

Up next are the *kubernetes-cli, the sql command line tools,* and the *Azure CLI*, which can be installed through the command in Listing 1-12.

Listing 1-12. Install script for kubectl, sqlcmd, and the Azure CLI

```
choco install kubernetes-cli -y
choco install sqlserver-cmdlineutils -y
choco install azure-cli -y
```

Note   This will install the latest version of the Kubernetes CLI. For the examples in this book, this is fine and what we want. Just be aware that this can cause potential issues when working with older Kubernetes Clusters.

Our last requirement is *azdata*. While it can't be installed through choco currently, Microsoft is providing a permalink that makes it easy enough to automate its installation as shown in Listing 1-13.

Listing 1-13. Install script for azdata

```
curl -o azdata.msi https://aka.ms/azdata-msi
msiexec /i azdata.msi /passive
```

Depending on which labs you'll be replicating, some of these tools may not be required. Given that they're all rather lightweight, we'd recommend installing them all anyway.

NFS

As we want our storage node to act as an NFS server, we need to install this as well. We're choosing a single-node NFS for ease of use. A production cluster should be using enterprise-class storage.

Open an SSH session into the *storage* node and save the contents of Listing 1-14 to a file called enable-nfs.sh.

Listing 1-14. enable-nfs.sh

```
#!/bin/bash
apt install -y nfs-kernel-server
groupadd mssql -g 10001
useradd -u 10001 mssql -g mssql
addgroup --gid 472 grafana
useradd -g 472 -u 472 grafana

mkdir -p /srv/exports/volumes/
chown -R mssql:mssql /srv/exports/volumes/
echo '/srv/exports 172.16.94.0/24(rw,sync,no_subtree_check,no_root_squash)'
> exports
chmod 644 exports
mv exports /etc/exports
exportfs -a
systemctl restart nfs-kernel-server

mkdir /srv/exports/volumes/sql-instance-1
chown -R mssql:mssql /srv/exports/volumes/
```

```
mkdir /srv/exports/volumes/influxdb
mkdir /srv/exports/volumes/grafana
chown 472:472 /srv/exports/volumes/grafana

mkdir /srv/exports/volumes/webcontent
echo "Hello World!!!" > /srv/exports/volumes/webcontent/index.html
```

This script will install the NFS server, create a directory for its contents (as well as some directories we'll use later for our first SQL Server deployment), and start the service. To run this script, you need to make it executable and run it as root as shown in Listing 1-15.

Listing 1-15. Run enable-nfs.sh

```
chmod +x enable-nfs.sh
sudo ./enable-nfs.sh
```

Your NFS server is now ready and accessible.

On the other machines, install the NFS utilities using the command in Listing 1-16. This needs to be executed on every other VM individually.

Listing 1-16. Install NFS utilities on NFS clients

```
sudo apt install -y nfs-common
```

Test the connection from any client machine by mounting the NFS share using the code in Listing 1-17 and listing its content.

Listing 1-17. Verify NFS connection on NFS clients

```
sudo mount -t nfs storage:/srv/exports /mnt
ls -al /mnt/volumes
```

The result from Listing 1-17 should look like what we see in Figure 1-1.

```
labuser@node1:~$ ls -al /mnt/volumes
total 20
drwxr-xr-x 5 10001 10001 4096 Mar  1 09:47 .
drwxr-xr-x 3 root  root  4096 Mar  1 09:47 ..
drwxr-xr-x 2   472   472 4096 Mar  1 09:47 grafana
drwxr-xr-x 2 root  root  4096 Mar  1 09:47 influxdb
drwxr-xr-x 2 10001 10001 4096 Mar  1 09:47 sql-instance-1
```

Figure 1-1. *NFS test from node1*

System Swap Settings

As our last step, let's ensure that swap is disabled on our Control Plane as well as the three nodes, as this is a requirement of the kubelet.

Open an individual SSH connection into each of them and run the command in Listing 1-18.

Listing 1-18. Disable swap

```
swapoff -a
```

Also remove any swap partitions from */etc/fstab*. If you created your VMs using our script in Azure, this is not required.

Summary

In this chapter, we have laid the foundation for the labs we will perform together throughout the book. We will start off with deploying SQL Server as a container in Docker. Then we'll move on to building our Kubernetes cluster together and deploying SQL Server and demo applications and databases in that cluster. In addition to the cluster, we also highlighted the tools needed for interacting with the applications and databases we will deploy in our cluster.

CHAPTER 2

Container Fundamentals

Containers are changing the way applications are deployed. In this chapter, we will begin with the benefits of container-based application deployment and lay a solid technical foundation of container fundamentals introducing operations such as creating and running containers and persisting data. The chapter will close with the need for container orchestrators and introduce Kubernetes and its benefits. The goal of this chapter is, if you have never seen a container before, to become proficient in container basics before moving on to container orchestration with Kubernetes.

Container-Based Application Deployment

A *container* is a form of operating system virtualization. For years now, database professionals have become familiar with the concepts of machine virtualization where operating systems are multiplexing the hardware resources of our physical servers, the CPU, memory, and disk. In containers, the underlying operating system, its kernel, and resources are being multiplexed, or shared by applications running on that system. Each container thinks it is the only process running on the operating system. The operating system, in turn, controls access to the underlying hardware as normal. We will explore this isolation concept in more detail shortly. The software that has the responsibility of coordinating this work with the underlying operating system is called a *container runtime.*

A container is a running *container image. A* container image contains the binaries, libraries, and file system components to run our application. So, when the container starts up, it will begin executing the defined executable inside it and then has access to the resources of the operating system, in terms of creating additional processes and performing disk or network I/O and so on. Figure 2-1 shows the relationship between a container and its application.

© Anthony E. Nocentino, Ben Weissman 2021
A. E. Nocentino and B. Weissman, *SQL Server on Kubernetes*, https://doi.org/10.1007/978-1-4842-7192-6_2

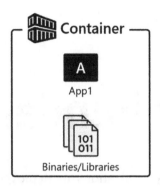

Figure 2-1. *A containerized application*

Conventionally, there is only one application inside a container, because the application is the unit of work and also our unit of scaling. When a container starts, it will begin executing a defined application inside it. There are scenarios where you can put multiple applications inside containers if there is a very tight relationship between those applications, for example, an application server and a metrics data collector.

Containers provide *isolation*. A process running inside a container cannot see any other processes running on the operating system or even processes running inside other containers. This concept is key to the portability and usability of and frankly the success of containers.

Containers also can tie specific libraries to an application, helping you solve application library conflicts. Have you ever had an application that needed to be installed on a dedicated server because it required a specific version of a DLL or library and that version conflicted with another version perhaps supporting a different application? Containers can save you from having to do that. If a container has the required libraries available inside the container image, when loaded, they are isolated to that running container. Additional containers can be started up with potentially conflicting libraries, and those container-based applications will happily run in isolation of each other.

The isolation from using containers provides portability in upgrading. You can upgrade a library inside a container without impacting other applications running in containers on your system. In Figure 2-2, you can see multiple application containers running on a physical or virtual machine sharing the base operating system. These containers' executions are completely isolated from each other. If they need to communicate, they must do so over the network.

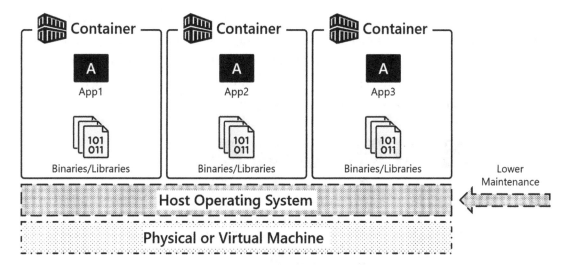

Figure 2-2. *Container-based application deployments*

Containers are *ephemeral*, and this ephemerality is one of the superpowers of containers. When a container is up and running, the container has state in terms of the actual program state and any file data changed inside it. A container can also be deleted, and when deleted. any program state and file data inside the container is deleted.

The ephemerality of containers is key to the concept of how container-based applications are deployed and maintained. Decoupling configuration and state from the container lifecycle itself is a core foundation of containers and also container orchestration. Techniques for decoupling configuration and state for containers are introduced later in this chapter with environment variables and Volumes and later in the book with Kubernetes constructs to help us achieve the same goals.

What's So Hard About Virtual Machines?

Virtual machines have been strongly seated in enterprise IT as the platform of choice for about the last 20 years. We challenge you, the reader, to think what did virtualizing hardware gain you in your data center. You got better utilization of your hardware... That's great. But what's the cheapest thing in your data center? Your hardware. What's the most expensive thing in your data center? You! Your time is the most expensive resource. When using virtual machines as our platform, there is little to no operational efficiency added to our organization, because virtual machines do not add to optimizing an organization's most expensive resource, the people.

Figure 2-3 is the traditional implementation of virtual machines in a data center. Operations teams build the infrastructure, install the guest operating systems, and install all the applications on top of those OSs, and that's the production environment. Operations teams very much so put an enormous amount of effort in keeping the systems and the applications properly functioning in this architecture.

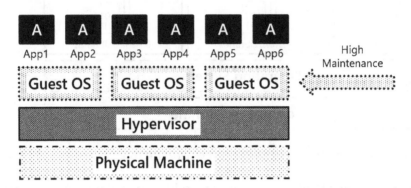

Figure 2-3. *A traditional implementation of VMs and their applications in an enterprise data center*

Here are some of the challenges of deploying applications with virtual machine–based platforms:

- **Operating system resource overhead:** Running VMs has an inherent CPU and memory overhead. This CPU time and memory could be better spent supporting applications rather than operating systems.

- **Operating system patching:** Updating operating systems adds very little business value to your organization. It certainly is required to maintain a proper security posture but does not move your business forward.

- **Troubleshooting:** For years and years, systems were built, rolled out into production, and were left alone. If something broke, IT operations had to put on their capes and fix the system.

- **Operating system upgrades:** We think the hardest thing in IT to do is upgrading an operating system, because if you upgrade your OS, what do you have to test? EVERYTHING! This tight coupling of application to OS means each time a change is made to the base OS, it injects risk into our system.

- **Deployments:** End-to-end automated deployments of VMs and their applications are rare in enterprise IT. Moreover, these solutions are often custom-built, point solutions, which can be hard to maintain.

Do any of the challenges of running virtual machine–based platforms mentioned move your business forward? Is anything gained by using virtual machines? We don't think so…and perhaps there's a better way.

Containers

When using container-based application deployments, containers directly attack some of the challenges identified when deploying applications on virtual machine–based platforms. Let's look at what containers bring to the table:

- **Speed:** When compared with VMs, containers are significantly smaller. For example, a virtual machine with SQL Server installed on Windows at a minimum will be 60+GB before you include any user databases. The current container image for SQL Server is about 1.5GB in size. Moving a 1.5GB container image around a modern data center is relatively trivial. Deploying a 60+GB VM can take some time.

- **Patching:** When it comes to patching an application, patching is a separate process from deployment. You'll likely need additional tooling to do so. Leveraging containers, you can very quickly update your application by simply pulling a new container image for your application and starting a new container up on that newer version of your application. If configuration and state are properly decoupled from the container, our app can pick up and start functioning again on the newer version with little to no impact on the application users.

- **Troubleshooting:** Due to the ephemerality of containers, a primary troubleshooting technique for container-based applications is to kill and redeploy the container. Since the container image is a known good starting point for our program's state, one can simply restart a container and get back into a good state.

- **Operating system upgrades:** When moving between versions of an operating system, a container can be deleted and recreated on the newer version of the OS. Since an application's required libraries are contained within the container, risk is reduced when moving between versions of the operating system.

- **Fast and consistent deployments:** When using container-based application deployment, deployments are written in code. Efficiencies are gained in how applications are deployed and maintained. In terms of speed, there is no longer a reliance on humans for the work and also consistency, since there is code that represents the state of the system, which can be used repeatedly in deployment processes. This code is placed into source control and is the configuration artifact for the desired state of the system.

Deployment automation is no longer going to be an afterthought or something to strive for in enterprise IT; it will be the primary way applications are deployed – using source-controlled code defining the desired state of the system. Container-based deployment techniques provide IT organizations the ability to provide services to the business more quickly and consistently and enable IT to maintain infrastructure and applications more easily, adding to organizations' operational efficiency. Application deployment and maintenance can get done faster and more confidently.

Both Docker and Kubernetes enable IT organizations to write code representing a system's desired state. This code can then be updated effecting the desired changes to applications, platforms, and systems. Code can be written for initial deployments, applying updates, and patching container-based applications. These techniques can also be used to enable troubleshooting with greater efficiency and if needed build self-healing applications. Each of these concepts will be further explored in much detail later in the book.

The Container Universe

OK, so now that you are familiar with the definition of a container and how it fits into modern application deployment processes, let's look at the container universe. There are a lot of emerging technologies and techniques, and we want to spend some time here familiarizing you with the names and players in this space.

The following list shows some of the names and players in the container universe:

- **Docker:** In today's container space, Docker is a technology more than anything. It is a container runtime and collection of tools that enables you to create and run container images and containers on an operating system, sharing the resources of that OS.

- **Docker Inc.:** This is the company that built the tooling and drove the technology to enable containers. Docker Inc. has open sourced the core technologies behind their container runtime and have spun off several open source projects such as *containerd* (*https://containerd.io/*), *Open Container Initiative* (*www.opencontainers.org/*), and more.

- **containerd:** Is a container runtime that coordinates the lifecycle functions of containers such as pulling container images and creating, starting, and stopping containers. containerd is used by Docker and Kubernetes among others to coordinate container lifecycle functions. In Kubernetes, the container runtime is a pluggable component. containerd is the de facto standard.

- **Other container runtimes:** The world of containers isn't all Docker on Linux. There are some other players in the game. Here is just a small sample of the other container runtimes available:

  - **Container Linux/CoreOS (rkt):** A purpose-built operating system that emphasizes container-based application deployment using an application container runtime called *rkt* (pronounced rocket, *http://coreos.com/*).

  - **Podman:** A container runtime for running Linux containers on Red Hat–based operating systems. For more information, visit *https://github.com/containers/libpod*.

  - **Windows Server 2016:** Gives you the ability to run both Windows and Linux containers. For more information, visit *https://docs.microsoft.com/en-us/virtualization/ windowscontainers/*.

Note   In this chapter, we will use Docker as the container runtime for our single-container deployment scenarios. In later chapters, we will use containerd as the container runtime in our Kubernetes Clusters.

Getting and Running Containers

Let's talk about what a *container image* is, how a container image is defined, and where container images live.

The following list highlights the key elements of container images:

- **Container image:** Contains the code, application binaries, libraries, and environment variables to run our application. In the most basic terms, these are the things needed to run our application. A running container image is called a container.

- **Docker file:** Defines the elements of a container image. It tells the container runtime which binary to start up when the container starts, which network ports to expose, and other critical information about the container image to be built.

- **Container registry:** This is where images are stored. Docker Hub is one of many container registries and is a primary place to store and exchange container images. Repositories are ways to organize container images within a container registry.

The Container Lifecycle

Following along in Figure 2-4, you'll see a container-based application's lifecycle. When a developer is ready, they will build their application in their normal application development platform. Then they will write a *Docker file* for that application. This Docker file contains the needed information to build a container image for that application. It will have information like which binary to start up when the container starts up and which network port the application lives on, among many other possible configuration attributes and instructions to build the image. Once the Docker file is ready, the developer will tell Docker to *build* an image. This will take the defined information from the Docker file and create a container image locally on the developer's workstation. That container image is then *pushed* (uploaded) into a *container registry* where it will sit until someone is ready to use that container image. When a user wants to start up a container from that container image, they will *pull* that container image down to their operating system, the container runtime on that OS will then create (run) a running container from the container image, and then the application is up and running in a container on that OS.

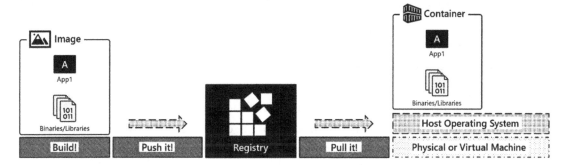

Figure 2-4. *A container lifecycle*

OK, so enough talk. Let's see how you can deploy SQL Server in a container on Docker. In this book, you will not be building container images. You will be using images available in public container registries. In this chapter, you will be working with SQL Server containers, and those images are available from the Microsoft Container Registry (*mcr.microsoft.com*).

Working with Container Images

To pull a container, execute the `docker pull` command and specify the container image you want to pull. In the following example, the container image is coming from the container registry `mcr.microsoft.com` from the repository `mssql/server,` and to ask for a specific container, you specify the *image tag*, which here is `2019-latest`. Listing 2-1 shows this command.

Listing 2-1. docker pull command for latest SQL Server 2019 image

```
docker pull mcr.microsoft.com/mssql/server:2019-latest
```

Figure 2-5 shows the resulting output of the command in Listing 2-1.

```
labuser@control:~$ docker pull mcr.microsoft.com/mssql/server:2019-latest
2019-latest: Pulling from mssql/server
04a5f4cda3ee: Pull complete
ff496a88c8ed: Pull complete
0ce83f459fe7: Pull complete
18147e02582b: Pull complete
32f0c0acc4b8: Pull complete
e036a29020fa: Pull complete
4ee3d995ce58: Pull complete
Digest: sha256:dde9e587abb7ca1a09e89b4ec4a48b36ab299bfbde1460c64e44ea9bdcb003ac
Status: Downloaded newer image for mcr.microsoft.com/mssql/server:2019-latest
mcr.microsoft.com/mssql/server:2019-latest
```

Figure 2-5. *Output of docker pull*

In the preceding example, a container image with the tag 2019-latest conventionally is being pulled. The maintainer of the container image repository defines a tag that points to the most recent version of their application by specifying a latest tag. If you want to pull a specific version of a container image, you will want to get a list of available tags from the repository. For SQL Server, you can do that with the commands shown in Listing 2-2 (Bash) and Listing 2-3 (Windows).

Listing 2-2. Command on Bash

```
curl -sL https://mcr.microsoft.com/v2/mssql/server/tags/list
```

Listing 2-3. Command on Windows

```
(Invoke-WebRequest https://mcr.microsoft.com/v2/mssql/server/tags/list).
Content
```

Figure 2-6 shows you a part of these commands' outputs. There are many more container images available, but we've omitted some for brevity.

```
{
  "name": "mssql/server",
  "tags": [
    "2017-CU1-ubuntu",
    "2017-CU10",
    "2017-CU10-ubuntu",
    "2017-CU11",
    "2017-CU11-ubuntu",
    "2017-CU12",
    "2017-CU12-ubuntu",
    "2017-CU13",
    "2017-CU13-ubuntu",
    "2017-CU14",
    "2017-CU14-ubuntu",
    "2017-CU15",
    "2017-CU15-GDR",
```

Figure 2-6. *Abbreviated list of container images and their tags*

If you want to pull a specific container, you need to specify a container image tag. The command in Listing 2-4 will pull the container image associated with the tag 2019-CU9-ubuntu-18.04.

Listing 2-4. docker pull command to pull container image associated with specific tag

```
docker pull mcr.microsoft.com/mssql/server:2019-CU9-ubuntu-18.04
```

To get a list of images available on a local system, execute the docker image ls command in Listing 2-5. The command's output shows the images that have been pulled to the local system. The following is an example.

Listing 2-5. docker image ls command

```
docker image ls
```

For each image, the output (Figure 2-7) shows the image's repository, the tags, the image identifier (the IMAGE ID), the creation date, and the image size.

```
REPOSITORY                           TAG                      IMAGE ID       CREATED        SIZE
mcr.microsoft.com/mssql/server       2019-latest              62c72d863950   5 weeks ago    1.49GB
mcr.microsoft.com/mssql/server       2019-CU9-ubuntu-18.04    a8948ed97d80   3 months ago   1.39GB
```

Figure 2-7. *Output of docker image ls command*

It is a common misconception that the creation date shown by the docker image ls command is the date on which the image was pulled. That's not the case. The creation date really is the date on which the image was created.

A container image can have multiple tags. In the preceding output, if you look closely at the container IMAGE ID, you will notice that both container images have the same value for IMAGE ID. The tags 2019-latest and 2019-CU9-ubuntu-18.04 point to the same container image because the latest image at the time of this writing for SQL Server 2019 is CU9. When a new container image is published into the repository, it will have a new, unique container image ID. The repository administrator will update the latest tag to point to this newest image in that repository.

Starting a Container

To start a container, execute the docker run command like in Listing 2-6, and let's walk through the following example.

Listing 2-6. docker run command

```
docker run \
    --env 'ACCEPT_EULA=Y' \
    --env 'MSSQL_SA_PASSWORD=SOmethingS@StrOng!' \
    --name 'sql1' \
    --publish 1433:1433 \
    --detach \
    mcr.microsoft.com/mssql/server:2019-CU9-ubuntu-18.04
```

To run SQL Server in a container, a couple things are required to configure SQL Server for its initial startup. As discussed earlier, decoupling configuration and state is key to running applications in containers. Here is an example of decoupling configuration. SQL Server exposes configuration points as environment variables. And you can inject configuration at runtime by specifying values for those environment variables. In the preceding command, you see --env 'ACCEPT_EULA=Y'. This specifies the value 'Y' for the environment variable ACCEPT_EULA. At startup, SQL Server will look for this value and start up accordingly. Similarly, defined is an environment variable 'MSSQL_SA_PASSWORD=SOmethingS@StrOng!'. This sets the sa password at container startup, which in this case is SOmethingS@StrOng!. While not required, a container name is specified with the `--name='sql1'` parameter, which is useful when working with containers at the command line and gives us the ability to address the container by its name.

Tip   For more information on configurations available as environment variables, check out *https://docs.microsoft.com/en-us/sql/linux/sql-server-linux-configure-environment-variables*.

In addition to application configuration and name, to access the container-based application over the network, a port must be exposed. The parameter `--publish` `1433:1433` exposes a port from inside the container to one outside the container on the base operating system. Let's unpack this a bit, as this is one place we tripped up often when we got started with containers. The first `1433` is the port on which the application is listening on the base operating system. By default, it will listen on the IP address of the host OS, so this is how users and other applications will access the container-based application either locally on the same host or remotely from other hosts. The second `1433` is the port listening "inside" the container. More on this later when in the discussion on container internals. Next is `--detach,` which tells the container runtime to detach the running process from standard out. This gives us control of our terminal back and runs SQL Server as a background process.

Note   If you are having trouble starting a container, remove the `--detach` parameter so you can see the container's log on the screen streamed to standard out. In SQL Server containers, this is the `SQL Server Error Log.` The most common reason we see when creating a container is the `sa` password is not complex enough; this will surface quickly when looking at the Error Log. `docker` `logs` is also helpful in this scenario.

And finally, the specific container image to start this container from, and in this example, it is `mcr.microsoft.com/mssql/server:2019-CU9-ubuntu-18.04`.

If the `docker run` command is successful, it will print the container ID to standard out.

Execute `docker ps` in Listing 2-7 to list the containers running on a local system.

Listing 2-7. docker ps command

```
docker ps
```

Figure 2-8 shows the command's output. The `sql1` container is up and running. It also shows the container ID, which container image it started from, the command started when the container started up, the container name, when the container was created, and the container's current status, which in this case has been up for 10 minutes.

```
CONTAINER ID   IMAGE                                             COMMAND                 CREATED         STATUS         PORTS                                          NAMES
777cc8d5480a   mcr.microsoft.com/mssql/server:2019-CU9-ubuntu-18.04   "/opt/mssql/bin/perm_"   47 seconds ago   Up 46 seconds   0.0.0.0:1433->1433/tcp, :::1433->1433/tcp   sql1
```

Figure 2-8. *List of containers running on a local system*

What If Something Goes Wrong?

Use the `docker logs` command combined with the container name (Listing 2-8), in this case `sql1`, to get the output from the container. In SQL Server, the output you'll find here is from the SQL Server Error Log, which will likely hold valuable information on why your container isn't starting up.

Listing 2-8. docker logs command

```
docker logs sql1 | more
```

Accessing a Container-Based Application

In this case, the application is SQL Server, so let's use the command line utility sqlcmd to access SQL Server. The code in Listing 2-9 shows a query to get the @@VERSION output.

Listing 2-9. Command line utility sqlcmd to access SQL Server

```
sqlcmd -S localhost,1433 -U sa -Q 'SELECT @@VERSION' -P 'SOmethingS@
StrOng!'
```

In Figure 2-9, you can see a container running SQL Server 2019 CU1, which matches what the container image specified at container startup.

```
Microsoft SQL Server 2019 (RTM-CU9) (KB5000642) - 15.0.4102.2 (X64)
        Jan 25 2021 20:16:12
        Copyright (C) 2019 Microsoft Corporation
        Developer Edition (64-bit) on Linux (Ubuntu 18.04.5 LTS) <X64>

(1 rows affected) _
```

Figure 2-9. Container image specified at container startup

Starting a Second Instance of SQL Server

To start a second instance of SQL Server 2019 CU1 as a container, you execute docker run again. The key differences will be a unique container name, in this case sql2, and also a unique port to publish on. In this case, the second SQL Server instance is available on port 1434 as displayed in Listing 2-10. To access this instance of SQL Server, applications will point to that port. In the following command, rather than use the full parameter names as we did in the previous docker run command, we are using abbreviated parameter names.

Listing 2-10. docker run command with unique container name

```
docker run \
    --name 'sql2' \
    -e 'ACCEPT_EULA=Y' \
    -e 'MSSQL_SA_PASSWORD=SOmethingS@StrOng!' \
    -p 1434:1433 \
    -d mcr.microsoft.com/mssql/server:2019-CU9-ubuntu-18.04
```

docker ps will again yield a list of the running containers.

The command's output in Figure 2-10 shows both containers up and running, sql1 and sql2.

CONTAINER ID	IMAGE	COMMAND	CREATED	STATUS	PORTS	NAMES
f21beb6627bf	mcr.microsoft.com/mssql/server:2019-CU9-ubuntu-18.04	"/opt/mssql/bin/perm..."	8 seconds ago	Up 4 seconds	0.0.0.0:1434->1433/tcp, :::1434->1433/tcp	sql2
777cc8d5480a	mcr.microsoft.com/mssql/server:2019-CU9-ubuntu-18.04	"/opt/mssql/bin/perm..."	4 minutes ago	Up 4 minutes	0.0.0.0:1433->1433/tcp, :::1433->1433/tcp	sql1

Figure 2-10. Output of docker ps command

Now that there are two containers up and running, let's restore a database into one of those containers. In the book downloads, you'll find a SQL Server database TestDB1.bak and a restore script restore_testdb1.sql.

The contents of restore_testdb1.sql can also be seen in Listing 2-11.

Listing 2-11. restore_testdb1.sql

```
USE [master]
RESTORE DATABASE [TestDB1]
FROM DISK = N'/var/opt/mssql/data/TestDB1.bak'
WITH REPLACE
```

Let's walk through the process of restoring a database, looking inside the container to see the file layout, and then go through the lifecycle of running a container.

Restoring a Database to SQL Server Running in a Container

The command in Listing 2-12 copies an existing database backup into a container at the directory /var/opt/mssql/data inside the sql2 container, and the command in Listing 2-13 then sets the appropriate permissions on that copied backup file.

Due to the nature of the non-root SQL Server container in SQL Server 2019 (*https://techcommunity.microsoft.com/t5/sql-server/non-root-sql-server-2019-containers/ba-p/859644*), the permissions of the file copied into the container need to be adjusted so the sqlservr process inside can read the file copied. On Linux systems, the command docker cp will copy the file as the UID of the user from the base operating system executing the docker cp command. The sqlservr process inside the container runs as the user mssql. The following chown command changes the ownership of the backup file to the user mssql so the user can read the file.

Listing 2-12. docker cp command

```
docker cp TestDB1.bak sql2:/var/opt/mssql/data
```

Listing 2-13. chown command inside the container

```
docker exec -u root sql2 chown mssql /var/opt/mssql/data/TestDB1.bak
```

With that file in the correct location, execute the restore_testdb1.sql script, which contains the required T-SQL to restore this database. Notice we're running this restore (Listing 2-14) from outside the container and using sqlcmd on a client workstation and pointing it to the correct server name (localhost) and port 1434.

Listing 2-14. Execute restore script through sqlcmd

```
sqlcmd -S localhost,1434 -U sa -i restore_testdb1.sql -P
'SOmethingS@StrOng!'
```

sqlcmd will confirm the successful restore as shown in Figure 2-11.

```
Changed database context to 'master'.
Processed 336 pages for database 'TestDB1', file 'TestDB1' on file 1.
Processed 2 pages for database 'TestDB1', file 'TestDB1_log' on file 1.
RESTORE DATABASE successfully processed 338 pages in 0.213 seconds (12.378 MB/sec).
```

Figure 2-11. *Successful restore of a database*

With the database restored, let's use the docker exec command in Listing 2-15 to get access to the inside of the container. This will allow us to explore the internals of our running container. The parameter -it gives you an interactive terminal for the process being executed, which in this case is /bin/bash, a bash prompt. In the following example, the prompt presented shows the username of the logged-in user, mssql, and the hostname of the container that matches the container ID of the container.

Listing 2-15. docker exec command

```
docker exec -it sql2 /bin/bash
```

With this interactive bash shell that is running inside the container, let's look around a bit. Execute a ps -aux command as shown in Listing 2-16 to list all processes running.

Listing 2-16. pa -aux command

```
ps -aux
```

In the output shown in Figure 2-12, you will see there is only a small set of processes running inside the container: two sqlservr processes, a bash shell, and the ps command. This example highlights the isolation a container has at runtime. This container and its running processes cannot see any other processes running on the base operating system.

```
USER       PID %CPU %MEM    VSZ    RSS TTY      STAT START    TIME COMMAND
mssql        1  0.3  0.5 139736 22932 ?        Ssl  12:54    0:00 /opt/mssql/bin/sqlservr
mssql        9  8.0 16.4 8906800 663804 ?      Sl   12:54    0:13 /opt/mssql/bin/sqlservr
mssql      180  1.5  0.0  18512   3304 pts/0   Ss   12:57    0:00 /bin/bash
mssql      189  0.0  0.0  34408   2760 pts/0   R+   12:57    0:00 ps aux
```

Figure 2-12. *Output of pa -aux command*

Now, execute the directory listing (Listing 2-17) with `ls -la /var/opt/mssql/data`. This is the default database directory for SQL Server on Linux.

Listing 2-17. Directory listing

```
ls -la /var/opt/mssql/data
```

As you can see in Figure 2-13, you will find the system and user databases in this directory. You will also find the database backup file you copied in the preceding demo, the `TestDB1.bak` file. Each container has a separate file system. So the files in this directory are only available to this running container. If this container is deleted, these files will be deleted with the container. We will introduce data persistency for containers shortly.

```
total 99020
drwxr-xr-x 2 mssql root       4096 May 10 12:56 .
drwxrwx--- 1 root  root       4096 May 10 12:54 ..
-rw-r----- 1 mssql root        256 May 10 12:54 Entropy.bin
-rw-rw-r-- 1 mssql 1000     458752 May 10 12:55 TestDB1.bak
-rw-r----- 1 mssql root    8388608 May 10 12:56 TestDB1.mdf
-rw-r----- 1 mssql root    8388608 May 10 12:56 TestDB1_log.ldf
-rw-r----- 1 mssql root    4194304 May 10 12:54 master.mdf
-rw-r----- 1 mssql root    2359296 May 10 12:56 mastlog.ldf
-rw-r----- 1 mssql root    8388608 May 10 12:54 model.mdf
-rw-r----- 1 mssql root   14090240 May 10 12:54 model_msdbdata.mdf
-rw-r----- 1 mssql root     524288 May 10 12:54 model_msdblog.ldf
-rw-r----- 1 mssql root     524288 May 10 12:54 model_replicatedmaster.ldf
-rw-r----- 1 mssql root    4194304 May 10 12:54 model_replicatedmaster.mdf
-rw-r----- 1 mssql root    8388608 May 10 12:54 modellog.ldf
-rw-r----- 1 mssql root   15532032 May 10 12:56 msdbdata.mdf
-rw-r----- 1 mssql root     786432 May 10 12:56 msdblog.ldf
-rw-r----- 1 mssql root    8388608 May 10 12:54 tempdb.mdf
-rw-r----- 1 mssql root    8388608 May 10 12:54 tempdb2.ndf
-rw-r----- 1 mssql root    8388608 May 10 12:54 templog.ldf
```

Figure 2-13. *Default database directory for SQL Server on Linux*

To exit this container, use the `exit` command and return to our base OS's shell.

Stopping a Container

A container running a daemon process like SQL Server will continue to run until it is told to stop. To stop a running container, execute the `docker stop` command in Listing 2-18 and specify the container name or the container ID. In the following example, the container `sql2` is being stopped. This will send a `SIGTERM` signal to the processes running inside the container to gracefully shut down.

Listing 2-18. docker stop command

```
docker stop sql2
```

Finding Containers on a Local System

At this point, there are two containers on the local system. One container is currently stopped, `sql2`, and one is still running, `sql1`. Now execute a `docker ps` command.

In the output (Figure 2-14), there is only one running container, sql1.

CONTAINER ID	IMAGE	COMMAND	CREATED	STATUS	PORTS	NAMES
777cc8d5480a	mcr.microsoft.com/mssql/server:2019-CU9-ubuntu-18.04	"/opt/mssql/bin/perm…"	8 minutes ago	Up 8 minutes	0.0.0.0:1433->1433/tcp, :::1433->1433/tcp	sql1

Figure 2-14. *Output of docker ps command. List of running containers*

To see all of the containers on a system regardless of their current state, stopped or running, execute the `docker ps -a` command in Listing 2-19.

Listing 2-19. docker ps -a command

```
docker ps -a
```

In the output displayed in Figure 2-15, both containers are listed, `sql1` and `sql2`. The key piece of information is the `STATUS` column. `sql1` is still up and running, as indicated by a status value `16 minutes ago`. For the other container, `sql2`, the status is `Exited (0) 33 seconds`; it is currently stopped. The `0` is the exit code from the application. A non-zero exit code indicates an error occurred inside the program; a zero (0) indicates a graceful shutdown.

Note   If you find a non-zero exit code, something went wrong, and you will want to use `docker logs` to investigate the issue for that container.

CONTAINER ID	IMAGE	COMMAND	CREATED	STATUS	PORTS	NAMES
f21beb6627bf	mcr.microsoft.com/mssql/server:2019-CU9-ubuntu-18.04	"/opt/mssql/bin/perm…"	4 minutes ago	Exited (0) 24 seconds ago		sql2
777cc8d5480a	mcr.microsoft.com/mssql/server:2019-CU9-ubuntu-18.04	"/opt/mssql/bin/perm…"	8 minutes ago	Up 8 minutes	0.0.0.0:1433->1433/tcp, :::1433->1433/tcp	sql1

Figure 2-15. *Output of docker ps -a command. List of all containers on the respective system*

Starting an Existing Container

Since the container is still on the system, it can be restarted with `docker start` (Listing 2-20) and then specifying the container name. All of the state and configuration will still be there for this container, so our system and user databases will be there when the container is started up again.

Listing 2-20. docker start command

```
docker start sql2
```

We can then use sqlcmd to list the databases in our instance as shown in Listing 2-21.

Listing 2-21. List databases using sqlcmd

```
sqlcmd -S localhost,1434 -U sa -Q 'SELECT name from sys.databases' -P
'SOmethingS@StrOng!'
```

In the output in Figure 2-16, `sql2` is started up again, showing the current databases on the system including the restored user database `TestDB1`.

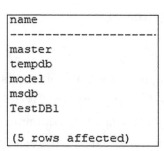

```
name
---------------------
master
tempdb
model
msdb
TestDB1

(5 rows affected)
```

Figure 2-16. *List of databases*

Now, let's clean up and stop these containers using Listing 2-22.

Listing 2-22. docker stop command

```
docker stop sql1
docker stop sql2
```

Removing a Container

When the containers are stopped, docker rm (Listing 2-23) will remove a container from a system. This is when the data inside the containers will be destroyed. So the restored TestDB1 is gone once these containers are removed. Data persistency independent of the lifecycle of the container is covered in the next section. In the following example, both sql1 and sql2 are deleted.

Listing 2-23. docker rm command

```
docker rm sql1
docker rm sql2
```

The preceding example deleted the containers, but not the container images. The container images are still on the local system and can be used to source new containers from. Executing docker image ls (Listing 2-24) shows the system the container images are on.

Listing 2-24. docker image ls command

```
docker image ls
```

In Figure 2-17, you can see the container images are still on the local system.

```
REPOSITORY                         TAG                      IMAGE ID       CREATED        SIZE
mcr.microsoft.com/mssql/server     2019-latest              62c72d863950   5 weeks ago    1.49GB
mcr.microsoft.com/mssql/server     2019-CU9-ubuntu-18.04    a8948ed97d80   3 months ago   1.39GB
```

Figure 2-17. *Output of docker image ls command. Container images on the local system*

Container Internals

Now, we want to take some time to look at container internals so that you can understand how the operating system implements and provides the isolation to processes and their resources when running inside containers.

A container is a running process with an isolated view of the underlying operating system and its resources. When a container is started from a container image, the container runtime is instructed to start a specific process that is defined in the container image. Also defined is which port the application is listening on, among other configuration information.

As shown earlier, a process listing executed inside the container shows only the processes running inside the container; no other processes on the system are visible. And even though the application is listening on port 1433 inside the container, to access the application, a unique port on the base operating system must be published... How can the operating system provide this isolation for our container-based applications on a single system? This is where Linux namespaces come in.

Namespaces

Linux kernel namespaces (*http://man7.org/linux/man-pages/man7/ namespaces.7.html*) are a kernel construct that provides isolation for processes running on Linux. There are six core namespaces available in Linux, five for resource isolation and one for resource governing. Looking at the following list of namespaces, you can get a feel for what namespaces provide. They provide isolation for programs and the resources the programs are using from the base operating system – things like processes, files, networking, and more.

The five resource isolation namespaces provide processes running on the system access to the services of the underlying operating system:

- **PID:** Process isolation

- **MNT:** File system and mountpoint isolation

- **NET:** Network device and stack isolation

- **IPC:** Interprocess communication

- **UTS:** Unique hostname and domain naming

The sixth namespace, cgroups, provides resource isolation for processes running on the base operating system. This enables multiple processes to run on the operating system and gives the administrator control over resource sharing:

- **cgroups:** Control Groups enable allocating and controlling access to system resources, like CPU, I/O, and memory.

For more information about how cgroups work, check out this link to the Linux man page: *http://man7.org/linux/man-pages/man7/cgroups.7.html*.

Union File System

A container image is read-only. When a container is running, any changes to files inside the container are written to a writeable layer using a copy on write technique. The Union File System takes the container image's base layer and the writeable layer and presents both back to the application as a single unified file system. This technique enables us to start many containers from a single image and gain the efficiencies of reusing that container image's layer as the starting point for many containers. Each container will have a unique writable layer that has a lifecycle tied to the container. When a container is deleted, this writable layer is deleted too. Which, if you are running a stateful application like SQL Server, does not sound too appealing. Techniques to provide data persistency to our container-based applications are coming up in the next section. The implementation details of Docker's Union File System have changed over the years from AUFS, UnionFS, and OverlayFS, but the implementation details are out of scope for this conversation.

Note   If you want to dig further into how container images work, we encourage you to check out our colleague Elton Stoneman's (@EltonStoneman) Pluralsight course "Handling Data and Stateful Applications in Docker" (*https://app. pluralsight.com/library/courses/handling-data-stateful-applications-docker/table-of-contents*).

Data Persistency in Containers

Containers are ephemeral, meaning when a container is deleted, it goes away…for good. In the preceding section, we introduced that as data changes inside a running container, it is written into a writeable layer and the Union File System has the responsibility of joining the layers together to present a single unified file system to the container-based application and when a container is deleted, the writeable layer is deleted as well. So can containers have data persistency across their lifecycle, from creation to deletion and creation again? You might also be asking, why would we need to delete a container?

Shouldn't we just be able to keep it up and running? Well yes, you can keep a container up and running, but if you need to change out the base container image (perhaps you have a new container image for your application due to an upgrade or some sort of patching), you will need to delete the existing container and start a new container using that new container image.

Docker Volumes

A Docker Volume (*https://docs.docker.com/storage/*) is a Docker managed resource that is independent of the lifecycle of the container. A Docker Volume allocates storage from the underlying operating system or shared storage and presents that storage into the container at a particular location inside the file system of the container.

Tip   Check out the Docker documentation for information on storage drivers by visiting *https://docs.docker.com/storage/storagedriver/*.

With a Volume mounted at a location inside the file system in the container, as the application changes data, it is written into that file system location and will be written to the Volume. This Volume is back-ended by storage that's outside of the container. Now if this container is deleted, the container and its writeable layer are still deleted, but the Volume remains since it has a lifecycle independent of the container. So all changes to other parts of the file system, not backed by a Volume, will not be persisted. But files written to the file location backed by the Volume will be persisted. If a new container is created and the Volume is mounted in the container, the data stored in the Volume is accessible inside the new container. Figure 2-18 shows a container-based application, sql1, accessing a Volume named sqldata1.

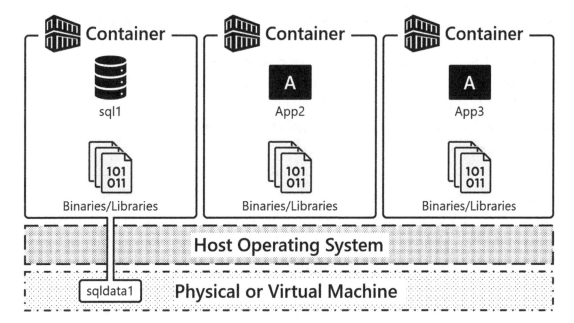

Figure 2-18. *A container with a Volume attached*

Let's look at some code to define a Docker Volume for a SQL Server container.

Creating a Container with a Volume

The code in Listing 2-25 shows a container starting up similar to our previous examples. The key difference is a data Volume is specified with the -v or --volume parameter.

Listing 2-25. docker run command – data Volume specification

```
docker run \
    --name 'sql1' \
    -e 'ACCEPT_EULA=Y' \
    -e 'MSSQL_SA_PASSWORD=S0methingS@Str0ng!' \
    -p 1433:1433 \
    -v sqldata1:/var/opt/mssql \
    -d mcr.microsoft.com/mssql/server:2019-CU9-ubuntu-18.04
```

Let's unpack that line of code there… -v specifies the configuration of a Volume. This creates a named Volume sqldata1, which will allocate a Volume from the underlying operating system's file system. The exact location is specific to the container runtime's platform, Windows, Linux, or MacOS. After the colon, you'll define where you want the Volume mounted inside the container, so this Volume is mounted at /var/opt/mssql, which is SQL Server's default instance directory in SQL Server on Linux containers. Inside this directory, you'll find the data files needed by SQL Server, such as the SQL Server Error Log, Trace files, Extended Event files, and system and user databases. Any data that's written into /var/opt/mssql is going to be written into the Volume, which is a resource independent of the container.

Note   SQL Server's binaries live in another part of the file system at /opt/mssql/bin. So, when a container image is replaced with a newer version of SQL Server, the new binaries will be used to start up the container, and our data will be read from /var/opt/mssql, which will persist between container instantiations.

So let's see this in action and run through a series of demos using SQL Server and Docker Volumes where the following key points will be highlighted. First, starting up a container with a Volume mounted at /var/opt/mssql inside the container and restoring a database. Next, deleting that container. Then, creating a new container that uses that same Volume and finally observing that our data persists independent of the lifecycle of this container. Let's get started.

In Listing 2-26, a container is defined with a Volume, sqldata1. This Volume is mounted in the file system of the container at /var/opt/mssql, so let's run this command.

Now, with the container up and running, copy a database backup into the container and set the appropriate permissions on the backup file. Then restore the database using the same process as the previous section. The code example (Listing 2-26) highlights these three steps.

Listing 2-26. docker cp command

```
docker cp TestDB1.bak sql1:/var/opt/mssql/data
docker exec -u root sql1 chown mssql /var/opt/mssql/data/TestDB1.bak
sqlcmd -S localhost,1433 -U sa -i restore_testdb1.sql -P
'SOmethingS@StrOng!'
```

sqlcmd will again confirm the execution.

With the container up and running and the user database restored, check out the list of current databases on this instance of our SQL Server container to confirm the database restore was successful (Listing 2-27).

Listing 2-27. List all databases through sqlcmd

```
sqlcmd -S localhost,1433 -U sa -Q 'SELECT name from sys.databases' -P
'SOmethingS@StrOng!'
```

In Figure 2-19, the output is shown. `TestDB1` is listed in the set of databases on this SQL Server instance.

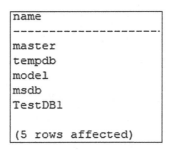

Figure 2-19. *List of databases on SQL Server instance*

This container has a Volume attached and mounted at `/var/opt/mssql` in its file system. When SQL Server starts up for the first time, it places critical instance files and system databases into this directory. The user database restored in the previous example is restored into the subdirectory `/var/opt/mssql/data` based on the code in the restore script (Listing 2-28).

Listing 2-28. List all files and their physical names through sqlcmd

```
sqlcmd -S localhost,1433 -U sa -Q 'SELECT name, physical_name from sys.
master_files' -P 'SOmethingS@StrOng!' -W
```

By querying `sys.master_files,` you can see (Figure 2-20) that all of the file locations for our databases are in `/var/opt/mssql/data,` which is contained within our Volume.

```
name physical_name
---- -------------
master /var/opt/mssql/data/master.mdf
mastlog /var/opt/mssql/data/mastlog.ldf
tempdev /var/opt/mssql/data/tempdb.mdf
templog /var/opt/mssql/data/templog.ldf
tempdev2 /var/opt/mssql/data/tempdb2.ndf
modeldev /var/opt/mssql/data/model.mdf
modellog /var/opt/mssql/data/modellog.ldf
MSDBData /var/opt/mssql/data/MSDBData.mdf
MSDBLog /var/opt/mssql/data/MSDBLog.ldf
TestDB1 /var/opt/mssql/data/TestDB1.mdf
TestDB1_log /var/opt/mssql/data/TestDB1_log.ldf

(11 rows affected)
```

Figure 2-20. *List of files and their locations*

Note   The default user database and log file locations are configurable as environment variables.

Check out *https://docs.microsoft.com/en-us/sql/linux/sql-server-linux-configure-environment-variables?view=sql-server-ver15* for more details on that. This topic will be examined further in Chapter 7.

The following commands will stop the container sql1 and remove it (Listing 2-29). This normally would destroy the data associated with this container...but it is now using a Volume.

Listing 2-29. Stop and remove the container sql1

```
docker stop sql1
docker rm sql1
```

Listing 2-30 creates a new container, and again it defines a Volume sqldata1. This is the same Volume used in the previous example and is a resource independent of the container, which you can see using the command docker volume ls. SQL Server's instance directory and its system and user databases are inside this Volume. So, when SQL Server starts up, it will find the master database in /var/opt/mssql/data and then read configuration and state of the instance. Any defined user databases that are available inside the file system will also be brought online.

Listing 2-30. docker run command – creation of new container

```
docker run \
    --name 'sql2' \
    -e 'ACCEPT_EULA=Y' \
    -e 'MSSQL_SA_PASSWORD=SOmethingS@StrOng!' \
    -p 1433:1433 \
    -v sqldata1:/var/opt/mssql \
    -d mcr.microsoft.com/mssql/server:2019-CU9-ubuntu-18.04
```

With the container up and running, query the current set of databases using the command in Listing 2-31.

Listing 2-31. List all databases through sqlcmd

```
sqlcmd -S localhost,1433 -U sa -Q 'SELECT name from sys.databases' -P
'SOmethingS@StrOng!'
```

And in the output, you can see TestDB1 (Figure 2-21). Now we do want to point out that it's not only user databases but also the system databases and the other files associated with the instance. So any configuration changes made to the instance will persist as well, for example, instance-level configurations such as Max Server Memory.

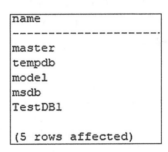

```
name
--------------------
master
tempdb
model
msdb
TestDB1

(5 rows affected)
```

Figure 2-21. *List of databases on SQL Server instance*

Our Volume is a resource independent of the container, and you can see that by using the docker volume ls command (Listing 3-32) as shown in the output.

Listing 2-32. docker volume ls command

```
docker volume ls
```

Figure 2-22 will show us all of the currently defined Volumes on our system.

```
DRIVER      VOLUME NAME
local       sqldata1  _
```

Figure 2-22. *List of Docker Volumes*

Looking Deeper into Volumes

Now when working with Docker, one of our favorite commands is `docker inspect`. This command as shown in Listing 2-33 is used to get more detailed information about a resource, and in the following example, executing `docker inspect` shows more detailed information about our Volume.

Listing 2-33. docker inspect command

```
docker volume inspect sqldata1
```

Let's walk through some of this output, which you can see in Figure 2-23. First is `CreateAt`, which is the date and time the Volume was created. Also available is the `Driver,` which is `local`. This means it is using the underlying operating system's file system. Next is `Mountpoint`; this is the actual path on the base operating system that's being exposed into the container. So, if you browse to this directory on the underlying operating system where the container is running, you will see the container's files inside of the Volume, and in our example here, you will find the SQL Server instance's files and its databases at this location.

```
[
    {
        "CreatedAt": "2021-05-10T13:16:23Z",
        "Driver": "local",
        "Labels": null,
        "Mountpoint": "/var/lib/docker/volumes/sqldata1/_data",
        "Name": "sqldata1",
        "Options": null,
        "Scope": "local"
    }
]
```

Figure 2-23. *Output of docker inspect – detailed information about Volume*

Note   If you're using Mac or Windows, these files are going to be abstracted away from you. Both Mac and Windows use virtualization technologies, so you can run Linux containers on those platforms. The actual file locations for these will be "inside" the VMs used to provide Linux kernel services to your container runtime. On a native Linux system running Linux containers, you will find these files at the actual file system location defined by Mountpoint.

Stopping and Removing Containers and Volumes

Now that we have highlighted the lifecycle of a container and also how to persist data externally from the container using a Volume, it is time to clean up our resources. We will now show you how to stop containers, delete containers, and also delete Volumes.

Executing `docker stop sql1` (Listing 2-34) tells the SQL Server process to stop and then stop the container.

Listing 2-34. docker stop command

```
docker stop sql1
```

To delete a container, use `docker rm` (Listing 2-35) and then the container name, `sql1`. Since its data is stored in a Volume, a new container can be created again if the desire remains to continue to work with that data.

Listing 2-35. docker rm command

```
docker rm sql1
```

But since this demonstration is complete, delete the Volume, with `docker volume rm sqldata1` (Listing 2-36). When the Volume is deleted, THIS is when the data will be destroyed. So use this with caution!

Listing 2-36. docker Volume rm command

```
docker volume rm sqldata1
```

Modern Application Deployment

Now that we have discussed core container fundamentals like how to start containers, access those applications, and persist data independent of the container's lifecycle, let's shift the conversation to how containers are used in modern application deployment scenarios and introduce the need for container orchestrators.

So far in this chapter, we have showed the configuration to start up a container, expose that application on the network, and also attach persistent storage to a container. But how is this done at scale in production systems? Do you want to be logging into servers and typing docker run each time you need to start up a container? Do you want to be tracking which ports your applications are listening/published on? No, implementing that configuration and also tracking what resources are where and how to access those is not a trivial task. This is where container orchestrators come into play.

Let's start off with an example application stack like the one in Figure 2-24.

SQL   Caching   Web 1

Web 2

Figure 2-24. *Example application architecture*

There are some basic questions on how this is deployed using containers:

1. How are these container-based applications deployed in our data center, and how are they started up?

2. Where do these container-based applications run in our data center and on which servers?

3. How do these container-based applications scale, and what if we wanted to scale from 2 to 20 web servers to support a burst in workload?

4. How do we consistently deploy this application stack?

5. How do we deploy this in another environment for testing or perhaps in another data center or cloud?

6. How do we or any of our applications access the services?

7. What IPs or DNS names are associated with these applications?

Container orchestrators help answer these questions.

The Need for Container Orchestrators

A container orchestrator is software that helps manage the deployment of your container-based applications. Container orchestrators are based on the core concepts of desired state and controllers. Container orchestrators will figure out where to run your workload in a collection of compute resources in your data center or cloud, start those containers up, and keep those containers up and running and in the defined state.

Let's introduce some of the key functionality of container orchestrators:

- **Workload placement:** Given a collection of servers in a data center, selecting which servers to run containers on.

- **Managing state:** Starting containers and also keeping them online. If something causes a container-based application to stop or become unavailable, a container orchestrator can react and restart the containers.

- **Speed and consistency of deployment:** Code is used to define application deployments. A container orchestrator will deploy what is defined in that code. This code is used to quickly and consistently deploy our applications.

- **Hide complexity in Clusters:** A container orchestrator exposes a programmatic API to interact with so users can be less concerned about the physical infrastructure for our applications and more focused on how applications are deployed.

- **Persistent application access endpoints:** A container orchestrator will track which services are available and provide persistent access to the services provided by our container-based applications.

There are several different container orchestrators available, and in this book, the focus is on Kubernetes (*https://kubernetes.io/*), as it has become the standard for open source container orchestrators. Therefore, the remainder of this book is focused on how to build a Kubernetes cluster and deploy SQL Server into that environment.

More Resources

For a deeper dive into Docker Volumes, check out Anthony's blog series "Persisting SQL Server Data in Docker Containers":

- *www.centinosystems.com/blog/sql/persisting-sql-server-data-in-docker-containers-part-1/*

- *www.centinosystems.com/blog/sql/persisting-sql-server-data-in-docker-containers-part-2/*

- *www.centinosystems.com/blog/sql/persisting-sql-server-data-in-docker-containers-part-3/*

Check out our technical reviewer and container expert Andrew Pruski's (*@dbafromthecold*) container blog series. If it has to do with containers, Andrew has likely blogged about it:

- *https://dbafromthecold.com/2017/03/15/summary-of-my-container-series/*

Also, make sure to take a look at the resources available by our good friend and all-around SQL Server expert Bob Ward (*@bobwardms*). SQL Server in containers is SQL Server on Linux. If you want to dive into how SQL Server on Linux works, be sure to check out Bob's book *Pro SQL Server on Linux*, which Anthony had the absolute pleasure of being the technical reviewer:

- **GitHub:** *https://github.com/microsoft/bobsql*

- ***Pro SQL Server on Linux:*** *www.apress.com/gp/book/9781484241271*

- ***SQL Server 2019 Revealed:*** *www.apress.com/gp/book/9781484254189*

Summary

Kubernetes is a container orchestrator, and in this chapter, we have laid the foundation of how containers work. We showed what a container is and how containers provide application isolation. Containers are used to quickly deploy applications, and in our examples, we ran SQL Server in a container. One of the key concepts in this chapter is the need to *decouple configuration and state* from a container's lifecycle, and the core tools for that are environment variables to inject configuration and Volumes to persist state (data) independently of a container's lifecycle. These are core concepts that will be revisited and leveraged throughout the remainder of the book as you learn how to deploy SQL Server on Kubernetes.

CHAPTER 3

Kubernetes Architecture

This chapter introduces Kubernetes, describing its role in modern application deployment, the benefits it provides, and its architecture. Starting off with its benefits, you will learn the value Kubernetes provides in modern container-based application deployment. Next, you will learn how the Kubernetes API enables you to build and deploy next-generation applications and systems. In that API, you will learn the core API primitives Kubernetes provides to define and deploy applications and systems. Then you will learn the key concepts of a Kubernetes cluster and its components and learn Kubernetes networking fundamentals.

Introducing Kubernetes

Kubernetes is a container orchestrator. It has the responsibility of starting up container-based applications on servers in a data center. To do this, Kubernetes uses *API Objects* representing resources in a data center, enabling developers and system administrators to define systems in code and use that code to deploy. Container-based applications are deployed as *Pods* into a *Kubernetes Cluster*. A Cluster is a collection of compute resources, either physical or virtual servers, called *Nodes*. Let's dive into each of these elements in more detail, starting with the benefits of Kubernetes and understanding the value it provides in modern application deployment:

- **Workload scheduling:** Kubernetes is a container orchestrator having the primary goal of starting up container-based applications, called Pods, on Nodes in a Cluster. It is Kubernetes' job to find the most appropriate place to run a Pod in the Cluster. When scheduling Pods on Nodes, a primary concern is determining if a Node has enough CPU and memory resources to run the assigned workload.

© Anthony E. Nocentino, Ben Weissman 2021
A. E. Nocentino and B. Weissman, *SQL Server on Kubernetes*, https://doi.org/10.1007/978-1-4842-7192-6_3

- **Managing state:** When code is deployed into Kubernetes, defining a workload that needs to be running, Kubernetes has the responsibility to start up Pods and other resources in the Cluster and keep the Cluster in the desired state. If the Cluster's running state skews from the desired state, Kubernetes will try to change the Cluster's running state to get the running state of the Cluster back into the defined desired state. For example, if a Deployment defines having a number of Pods running, if a Pod fails, Kubernetes will deploy a new Pod into the Cluster, replacing the failed Pod, ensuring the number of Pods defined by the Deployment are up and running. Further, suppose you want to scale the number of Pods supporting an application to add more capacity. In that case, you increase the number of replicas in the Deployment, and Kubernetes will create additional Pods in the Cluster ensuring the desired state is realized. More on this in the upcoming section on Controllers.

- **Consistent Deployment:** Deploying applications with code enables repeatable processes. The code defining a deployment is the configuration artifact and can be placed in source control. You can also use this code to deploy identical systems in down-level environments such as development environments or even between on-premises systems and the cloud. More on this in the upcoming section on the Kubernetes API.

- **Speed:** Kubernetes enables fast, controlled deployments, starting Pods in a cluster quickly. Furthermore, in Kubernetes, applications can be scaled quickly. Expanding the number of Pods supporting an application can be as simple as changing a line of code, and this can take as little as seconds. This will be demonstrated in great detail in Chapters 5 and 7.

- **Infrastructure abstraction:** The Kubernetes API provides an abstraction or wrapper around the resources available in a Cluster. When deploying applications, there is less focus on infrastructure and more on how applications are defined and deployed and consume the Cluster's resources. The code used for deployments will describe how the Deployment should look, and the Cluster will make that happen. If applications need resources such as public IP addresses or storage, that becomes part of the Deployment, and the Cluster will provision these resources for the applications' use.

- **Persistent Service endpoints:** Kubernetes provides persistent IP and DNS naming for applications deployed in the Cluster. As Pods can come and go due to scaling operations or reacting to failure events, Kubernetes provides this networking abstraction for accessing these applications. Depending upon the type of Service used, the service load balances application traffic to the Pods supporting the application. As Pods are created and destroyed, either based on scaling operations or in response to failures in the Cluster, Kubernetes automatically updates the information on which Pods provide the application services.

The Kubernetes API

The Kubernetes API provides a programmatic layer representing the resources available in a data center. The API enables you to write code to consume those resources in your application deployments. When writing code to consume the API, you use *API Objects*, which you use to define and deploy application workloads in Kubernetes. The code you write is submitted to the *API Server*. The API Server is the core communication hub in a Kubernetes Cluster. It is the primary way you interact with a Kubernetes Cluster and the only way Kubernetes components inside a Cluster exchange information. With the new Cluster state defined, either on initial Deployment or modifying an existing deployment, Kubernetes begins to implement the state described in your code. The desired state of your code becomes the running state in the Cluster.

API Objects

Kubernetes API Objects represent resources available in a Cluster. There are API Objects for compute, storage, and networking elements, among others, available in a Cluster for consumption by your application workloads. You will write code using these API Objects to define the desired state of your applications and systems deployed into a Kubernetes

Cluster. These defined API Objects communicate to the Cluster the desired state of the workload deployed, and the Cluster has the responsibility of ensuring that desired state becomes the running state of the Cluster.

We will now introduce the core API Objects to define workloads in a Kubernetes Cluster. These are the core building blocks of applications deployed in Kubernetes. In the upcoming sections, we will dive deeper into each of these individually:

- **Pods:** These are container-based applications. A Pod is the unit of work in a Cluster. A Pod is an abstraction that encompasses one or more containers and the resources and configuration it needs to execute, including networking, storage, environment variables, configuration files, and secrets.

- **Controllers:** These define and keep application workloads in the Cluster in the desired state. Some Controllers have the responsibility of starting Pods and keeping those Pods in the desired state. There are several different types of Controllers for ensuring the state of applications and systems deployed and also for the running state of the Cluster. We introduce several Controllers in this section and more throughout the book's remainder.

- **Services:** These provide a networking abstraction for access to Pod-based applications. Services are how applications' consumers, such as users and other applications, access the container-based application services deployed in a Cluster.

- **Storage:** Kubernetes provides abstractions for Pods to access storage and configuration data in a Cluster. Storage objects like the Persistent Volume and Persistent Volume Claim (PVC) are used to persist application data independent of the lifecycle of Pods.

- **Configuration data:** Configuration data can be stored in the cluster as *ConfigMaps* and *Secrets,* which can be exposed as files and environment variables to applications running in Pods.

In addition to the API Objects described, there are many more used to craft workloads, but these are the core API Object types focused on in this book and for deploying SQL Server.

API Server

The API Server is the central communication hub in a Kubernetes Cluster. It is the primary way users of Kubernetes interact with a Cluster to deploy workloads. It is also the primary way Kubernetes exchanges information between the components inside a Cluster. The API Server is a REST API available over HTTPS exposing API Objects as JSON. As Cluster users define workloads and communicate the information to the API Server, this information is serialized and persisted in a Cluster data store. Kubernetes then will move the running state of a Cluster into the desired state defined in those API Objects stored in the Cluster store.

Note   The Cluster data store is a pluggable resource. The dominant Cluster data store in Kubernetes is a distributed key-value store called etcd (`https://etcd.io/`).

Core Kubernetes API Primitives

Now it is time to look more closely at each of the high-level API Objects introduced in the last section. This section introduces Pods, Controllers, Services, storage, ConfigMaps, and Secrets. You will learn more details about each and how they enable you to deploy applications in Kubernetes and the workloads that each API Object allows you to deploy.

Pods

A Pod is also the most *basic unit of work* in a Kubernetes Cluster. At its core, a Pod is an API Object that represents one or more *containers*, its *resources* such as networking, storage, and *configuration* controlling its execution. Most commonly, a Pod API Object definition consists of the container image(s), networking ports used to talk to the container-based application, and, if needed, storage.

A Pod is the *unit of scheduling* in a Kubernetes Cluster. In Kubernetes, scheduling determines on which Node in a Cluster to start a Pod. Once the Pod is scheduled on the Node, a container using the specified container image is started on that Node by the container runtime, which conventionally is the Docker container runtime. When scheduling Pods on Nodes, Kubernetes ensures the resources like CPU and memory required to run the Pod are available on the selected Node and, if configured in the Pod, access to the storage.

Note   Kubernetes implements the Container Runtime Interface (CRI), meaning the container runtime is a pluggable resource and can use other CRI-compliant container runtimes. The de facto standard is containerd. See Chapter 2 for more details on this.

A Pod is the *unit of scaling*. When deploying applications in Kubernetes, you can scale an application horizontally by creating multiple copies of a Pod in a Cluster, called *Replicas*. Scaling Pod Replicas enables applications to support larger workloads by starting more containers on the Nodes in a Cluster and leveraging additional Cluster capacity. Further, running multiple Replicas of a Pod in a Cluster across multiple nodes provides high availability in the event of Pod or Node failures.

A Pod is *ephemeral*. If a Pod is deleted, its container(s) on the Node is stopped and then deleted. It is destroyed forever, including its writeable layer. A Pod is never redeployed. Instead, Kubernetes creates a new Pod from the current Pod API Object definition. There is no state maintained between these two deployments of a Pod. For stateless workloads, like web applications, this is OK. As new Pods are created, they can begin accepting workload when ready. But for stateful workloads like relational database systems, a Pod needs the ability to persist the state of the data stored in its databases independent of the Pod lifecycle. Kubernetes gives us API Objects and constructs for persistent storage, which are described in the following.

Controllers

Controllers define, monitor, and keep workloads and the running state of the Cluster in the desired state. This section focuses on Controllers for creating and managing Pods. In Kubernetes, it is rare to create Pods by defining and deploying a Pod Object manually. Two common Workload API objects are used for deploying applications in Kubernetes. They are *Deployment* and *StatefulSet*.

A Deployment is an API Object that enables you to define an application's desired state in the Pod's configuration and includes the number of Pods to create, called Replicas. The Deployment Controller creates a *ReplicaSet*. The ReplicaSet is responsible for starting Pods in the Cluster, using the Pod specification from the Deployment Object. The first frame of Figure 3-1 shows a Deployment that creates a ReplicaSet, and that ReplicaSet starts three Pods in the Cluster.

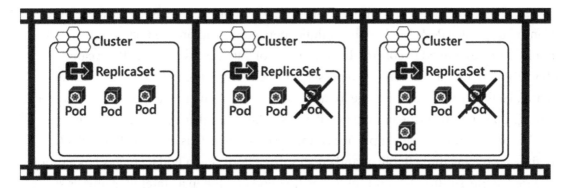

Figure 3-1. *ReplicaSet operations*

Controllers are responsible for keeping the running state of the Cluster in the desired state, so let's see that in action. In the second frame of Figure 3-1, let's say one of those Pods fails for any reason. Perhaps the application crashed, or maybe even the Node that Pod is running on is no longer available. In the third frame, the ReplicaSet Controller senses that the running state has deviated from the desired state and initiates the creation of a new Pod, ensuring the ReplicaSet, or the application, stays in the desired state of three Pods running at all times.

You might be asking, why does the Deployment Controller create a ReplicaSet rather than the Deployment creating the Pods directly? The Deployment Controller defines both the number of Pods to create and the Pod's configuration. When a Deployment configuration is updated, Pods in the old ReplicaSet shut down, and Pods in a new ReplicaSet are created. This enables the rollout of new container images or Pod configuration. A single Deployment Object still exists, and it manages the declarative updating and transitioning between ReplicaSets. If you want to dig deeper into this topic, check out the Pluralsight course "Managing Kubernetes Controllers and Deployments."

Deployment Controllers do not guarantee order or persistent naming of Pods. A Deployment consists of a collection of Pods, each of which is an exact copy of an application. However, a Pod's name is not persistent if a Pod is destroyed, and a new Pod is created in its place. Applications such as database systems often distribute data across multiple compute elements and then have to keep track of the data's location in the system for subsequent retrieval. Using a Deployment Controller can be problematic for stateful applications that require knowing the precise location of data in a collection of named compute resources.

To allow Kubernetes to support these types of stateful applications, the StatefulSet Controller creates Pods, each with a unique, persistent, and ordered name. So applications that need to control the placement of data across multiple Pods can do that as Pod names are ordered and persist independent of the Pod lifecycle. Further, StatefulSets provide stable storage for applications, ensuring the mapping of the correct storage object to the same named Pod if it has to be created again for any reason.

Figure 3-2 shows an example of a running StatefulSet. This example StatefulSet is defined as having three Replicas and creates three Pods. Each Pod it creates has a unique ordered name, sql-0, sql-1, and sql-2. The first Pod created in a StatefulSet always starts with a 0 index. In this example, that's sql-0. For each Pod added to the StatefulSet, the index is increased by one. So the next Pod is sql-1, followed by sql-2. If the StatefulSet is scaled up to add one more Pod, the next Pod is named sql-3. If the StatefulSet is scaled down, then the highest numbered Pod is removed first. In this example, sql-3 is removed. These ordered creation and scaling operations are essential to stateful applications that place data on named compute resources enabling the stateful applications to know the location of data at any point in time.

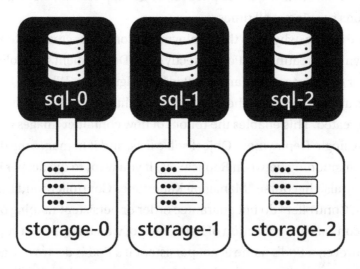

Figure 3-2. *An example StatefulSet – each Pod has a unique, ordered, and persistent name. Each Pod also has persistent storage associated*

There are many more controllers available in Kubernetes. This book focuses on Deployments, ReplicaSets, and StatefulSets and how they are used to deploy SQL Server on Kubernetes. There are controllers to help craft many different types of application workloads in Kubernetes. For more information on different controller types and their functions, check out the Kubernetes documentation at *https://kubernetes.io/docs/ concepts/workloads/.*

Services

As we introduced earlier, no Pod is ever recreated. Every time a Pod is created, either during its initial creation or when replacing an existing pod, that new Pod is assigned a new IP at startup. With controllers creating and deleting Pods based on configuration, or responding to failures, and affecting the desired state, this leaves us with a challenge of which IP address should be used to access application services provided by Pods running in a Cluster if they are constantly in flux.

Kubernetes provides a networking abstraction for access to Pod-based applications deployed in a Cluster called a *Service*. A Service is a persistent IP address and optionally a DNS name for access into an application running on Pods in a Cluster. Generally speaking, you will have one Service per application deployed in a Cluster. Application traffic received on the Service's IP is load balanced to the underlying Pod IP addresses. As Pods are created and destroyed by Controllers, such as a ReplicaSet Controller, the network information is automatically updated to represent the application's current state. Let's look at an example of this.

In Figure 3-3, let's say a Deployment creates a ReplicaSet, and the ReplicaSet creates three Pods. Each of those Pods has a unique IP address on the network. For users or applications to access the applications in those Pods, a Service is defined. A Service exposes the applications running in a collection of Pods on a persistent IP address and port, port 80 for HTTP. Users or other applications can access the application provided by that Service by connecting to the Service IP address or DNS name. The Service then load balances that traffic among the Pods that are part of the Service.

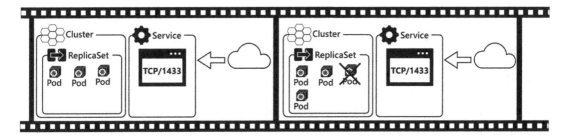

Figure 3-3. *ReplicaSet and Services*

In the second frame of Figure 3-3, let's say one of the Pods in the ReplicaSet fails. The ReplicaSet Controller senses this and deploys a new Pod and registers that new Pod's IP address in the Service and starts load balancing to the new Pod. The Pod that fails is deleted, and its IP address is removed from the Service, and traffic is no longer sent to that IP. This all happens automatically without any user interaction.

Further, when scaling an application up and adding more Pods or scaling an application down by removing some Pods, the Pod IPs are added or removed to or from the Service accordingly. It truly is a fantastic piece of technology, and we get very excited when we see this in action. This will be demonstrated in detail in Chapter 5.

There are three types of Services available in Kubernetes, all of which can be used to access applications running in Kubernetes. The service types are *ClusterIP*, *NodePort*, and *LoadBalancer*. Let's look at each in more detail:

- **ClusterIP:** ClusterIP Services are available *only* inside the Cluster. This type of Service is used when an application does not need to be exposed outside the Cluster.

- **NodePort:** A NodePort Service exposes your application on each Node's real IP address in your Cluster on a fixed port. NodePort Services are accessed using the real network IP addresses of Cluster Nodes combined with the service port. Received traffic is routed to the appropriate Pods supporting the Service. NodePort Services are used when Cluster-based applications need to be accessed outside the Cluster or integrated with external load balancers.

- **LoadBalancer:** This service type integrates a cloud provider's load balancer service or a cluster external load balancer deployed on-premises such as an F5. A LoadBalancer Service is used in cloud-based scenarios when cluster-based applications need to be accessed outside the Cluster.

Each of these Service types will be demonstrated in detail in Chapter 5.

Storage

As SQL Server professionals, our number one job is keeping data around. And Kubernetes has API Objects to enable the deployment of stateful applications, like SQL Server. There are two primary API Objects available to help with this, Persistent Volumes and Persistent Volume Claims. A Persistent Volume is storage available in a cluster defined by a cluster administrator available for consumption by Pods. There are many different types of storage available as Persistent Volumes, such as virtual disks from cloud providers, iSCSI, NFS, and many more. But Pods do not access the Persistent Volume object directly. A Pod uses a Persistent Volume Claim in the Pod Object definition to access cluster storage. The Persistent Volume Claim will "ask" the cluster for storage, and then the PVC will make a claim on the Persistent Volume and map the Persistent Volume to the Pod. This extra layer of abstraction decouples the Pod from storage implementation details of the Persistent Volume. This has the primary benefit of not having storage implementation details, such as infrastructure-specific storage parameters, as part of the Pod's definition. The implementation details are in the Persistent Volume object. Persisting data in Kubernetes will be covered in greater detail in Chapter 6.

ConfigMaps

In Kubernetes, application configuration data can be stored in the cluster as API Objects. A ConfigMap is an API Object that stores key-value pairs as data is a cluster resource. The stored data can be exposed to Pods and their containers as environment variables or even configuration files that the applications running in the containers can use for configuration. These are commonly used to configure more complex applications deployed in Kubernetes. ConfigMaps enable you to decouple the configuration from the code in the deployment manifest and store it in the cluster for reference at runtime. You will see ConfigMaps in use in Chapter 8.

Secrets

A Secret is an API Object used to store sensitive information to be used by applications deployed in your Kubernetes cluster. Secrets are commonly used to store things like passwords, API tokens, public and private key pairs, and TLS certificates. You can write a deployment manifest and refer to that Secret by name, and the information stored in the Secret can be exposed to the containers running in the Pods as environment variables or as files in the file system.

Secrets enable you to have safer and more flexible manifests and container images since you are not storing sensitive information along with those resources. You want to avoid storing sensitive information in deployment manifests and container images. Secrets allow you to store this type of potentially sensitive information in the cluster and retrieve it for later use at deployment time.

Kubernetes Cluster Components

The first part of this chapter introduces Kubernetes concepts and the core API Objects used to build and deploy workloads in a Kubernetes Cluster. Now it is time to dive into what a Kubernetes Cluster is, looking closely at each of the major components.

Exploring Kubernetes Cluster Architecture

A Kubernetes Cluster is a collection of servers (physical or virtual) called *Nodes* that provide a platform for running container-based applications in Pods. There are two types of Nodes in a Cluster. *Control Plane Nodes* are the controller of the Cluster itself, the brains behind the operations. *Worker Nodes* are the compute devices used to run Pods. Let's look at each more closely, starting with the Control Plane Nodes. Figure 3-4 provides us an overview of the cluster components.

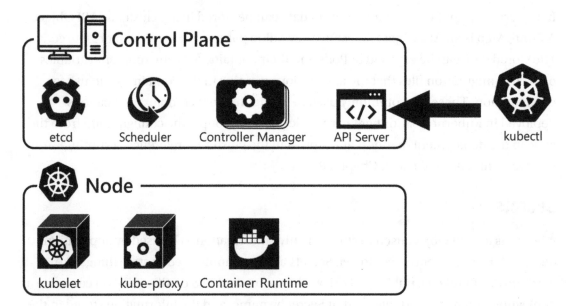

Figure 3-4. Kubernetes Cluster components

Control Plane Nodes

Control Plane Nodes operate the Control Plane Services. The Control Plane Services implement the core functions of a Kubernetes Cluster, such as managing the Cluster itself and its resources and controlling workload. The Control Plane consists of four components, each with a specific responsibility in the Cluster. They are the *API Server*, *etcd*, the *Scheduler*, and the *Controller Manager*. The Control Plane Services and Control Plane components are most commonly deployed as Pods that can run on a single Control Plane Node or run on several Control Plane Nodes for high availability. For more information on building highly available Clusters and their configuration, check out *https://kubernetes.io/docs/setup/production-environment/tools/kubeadm/high-availability/* and *https://kubernetes.io/docs/setup/production-environment/tools/kubeadm/ha-topology/*.

Let's look at each of the Control Plane functions and their responsibility in the cluster in more detail:

- **API Server:** The API Server is the main communication hub in a Cluster. All Cluster components communicate through the API Server to exchange information and state. It is a simple, stateless REST API that implements and exposes the Kubernetes API for access to users and other Cluster components. As API Objects are created, modified, or deleted, those objects' state is committed to the Cluster. Multiple replicas of the API Server can be deployed across several Control Plane Nodes, and API traffic can be load balanced for high availability.

- **Etcd:** etcd is a key-value data store used to persist the state of the Cluster. The API Server itself is stateless but serializes and stores object data in etcd. Since it does persist data, this needs to be protected for both recovery and availability. Backups of etcd should occur frequently, and if high availability is required, multiple replicas are configured in a highly available configuration.

- **Controller Manager:** The Controller Manager implements and ensures the desired state of the Cluster and its workloads. It uses control loops to monitor the running condition continually, compare it with the desired state, and make the changes needed to get the Cluster back into the desired state. To do this, the Controller Manager watches and updates the API Server. Earlier in this chapter, we introduced the concept of Controllers and how they enable you to tell the Kubernetes API what the desired state is. The Controller Manager implements that state. When it comes to Pods and application workloads, if a Deployment defines that three Pod Replicas of an application need to be online, the Controller Manager has the responsibility to ensure that those Pods are always online and ready reconciling the defined state with the Cluster's running state by creating new Pods if needed.

- **Scheduler:** The Scheduler decides which Node in a Cluster to start a Pod on. It monitors the API Server looking for any unscheduled Pods. If the Scheduler finds any unscheduled Pods, it determines the best place to run those Pods in the Cluster. The scheduling decision is based on the resources available in the Cluster, the requirements defined for each pod, and potentially any administrative policy constraints. If you would like more details on scheduling, please check out the Pluralsight course "Configuring and Managing Kubernetes Storage and Scheduling."

Worker Nodes

Worker Nodes run user application workloads. A cluster usually consists of at least one Control Plane Node and a collection of Worker Nodes. Each Worker Node contributes some amount of CPU and memory resources to the overall available resources in a Cluster. You will need enough CPU and memory resources to run your application workload in a Cluster, ensuring enough capacity for applications and also in the event of Node failures and even growth.

Note   A primary concern for the Control Plane Node is ensuring availability. Check out *https://kubernetes.io/docs/setup/production-environment/ tools/kubeadm/ha-topology/* for more information on high-availability Control Plane topologies.

All Nodes in a Cluster, either Control Plane or Worker, consist of three components, the *kubelet* that communicates with the API Server for Cluster operations, the *kube-proxy* that exposes containers running on a Node to the local network, and the *container runtime* that starts and runs the containers on the Node:

- **kubelet:** The kubelet is a service running on a Node and is responsible for communicating with the API Server, starting pods on a node, and ensuring that the Pods on that Node are in a healthy state. The kubelet monitors the API Server for Pod workload state, telling the container runtime to start and stop containers. It also reports back to the API Server the current state of Pods running on a Node and implements health checks on Pods in the form of Liveness Probes and Readiness Probes. The kubelet reports back to the API Server the Node's current state and the resources available on that Node.

- **kube-proxy:** kube-proxy is a container running on all Nodes in a Cluster and functions as a network proxy responsible for routing traffic from the network the Node is on to the Pods running on that Node.

- **Container runtime:** The container runtime is responsible for pulling container images and running containers on the Node. Today, most commonly, Docker is the container runtime used in Kubernetes Clusters. But the container runtime space is moving toward the Container Runtime Interface standard, which enables several different container runtimes to be used as the container runtime in Kubernetes Nodes. Kubernetes supports Docker, containerd, and CRI-O container runtimes. In this book, the container runtime used is Docker. See *https://kubernetes.io/docs/ setup/production-environment/container-runtimes/* for more information on the container runtimes supported in Kubernetes.

Networking Fundamentals

The final major topic in our Kubernetes primer chapter is networking. The Kubernetes networking model enables workloads to be deployed in Kubernetes while abstracting away network complexities. This simplifies application configuration and service discovery in a cluster and increases the portability of deployment code by removing infrastructure-specific code. This section introduces the Kubernetes networking model and example cluster communication patterns.

Three rules govern Kubernetes networking. These rules enable the simplicity described earlier. These rules are from *https://kubernetes.io/docs/concepts/cluster-administration/networking/*.

Kubernetes Networking Model Rules

1. All Pods can communicate with each other on all Nodes without Network Address Translation (NAT).

2. All agents, such as system daemons and the kubelet, on a Node can communicate with all Pods on that Node.

3. Pods in the host network of a Node can communicate with all Pods on all Nodes without NAT.

The preceding rules simplify networking and application configuration by ensuring Pods are talking to each other on the actual Pod IPs and container ports rather than having them translated to an IP scheme dependent upon the network infrastructure where they are deployed.

In Kubernetes, a Pod Network is the network Pods are attached to when the container runtime starts them on a Node. Each Pod deployed is given a unique IP address on the Pod Network. Pod Networks must follow the rules defined earlier, which results in Pods using their real IP addresses. When implementing Pod Networks, there are many solutions to ensure adherence to the Kubernetes networking model rules. A common solution is overlay networking, which uses a tunneling protocol to exchange packets between Nodes independent of the underlying physical infrastructure's network. This enables the overlay network to use a layer 3 IP scheme independent of the data center's physical infrastructure, enabling simpler adherence to the Kubernetes networking model.

Another option is to build a Pod Network as part of a data center infrastructure as part of a bare-metal approach. This will require the coordination of the Kubernetes Cluster administrator and the network engineering team responsible for the network.

The following are common communication patterns used in a Kubernetes Cluster showing Pods accessing each other and also accessing the Services provided by Pods.

Communication Patterns

Figure 3-5 shows some example communication patterns in a Kubernetes cluster. Let's walk through each of those together:

1. **Inside a Pod**

   Multiple containers within a Pod share the same container namespace. These containers can communicate with each other over localhost on unique ports.

2. **Pod to Pod within a Node**

   When Pods on the same Node need to communicate over the network, they do so over a local software bridge defined on the Node and use the Pod IP.

3. **Pod to Pod on another Node**

   When Pods on different Nodes need to communicate over the network, they do so over the local layer 2 or layer 3 network using the Pod IP.

4. **Services**

   When accessing Services in a cluster, traffic is routed to the kube-proxy implementing the Service and then routed to the Pod providing that application service. As introduced earlier in this chapter, Services will be your most common interaction with applications deployed in a Cluster.

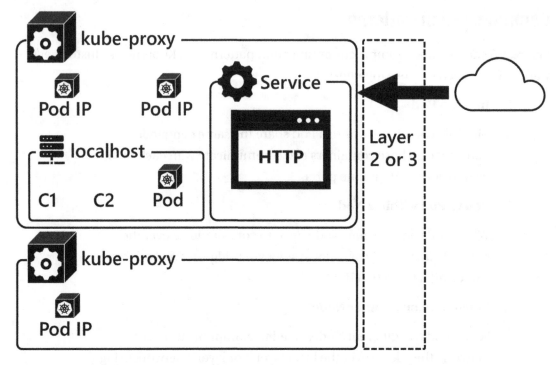

Figure 3-5. *Kubernetes networking*

Summary

This chapter introduced Kubernetes and how it enables deployment of modern container-based applications. You learned how the Kubernetes API enables you to build and model applications that are deployed into a Kubernetes Cluster. You also learned the core API primitives for deploying workloads: *Pods*, your container-based application; *Controllers*, keeping the cluster and its workload in the desired state; *Services*, for access to the applications; and *storage*, for stateful applications. Then you learned about the components of a cluster and how they work together to ensure that your desired state is implemented, and we had a quick tour of the Kubernetes networking model. With all that theory behind us, now it's time to move on to the next chapter where we will show you how to build a Kubernetes cluster and get a basic workload up and running.

PART II

Kubernetes in Practice

CHAPTER 4

Installing Kubernetes

In this chapter, we will introduce how to build a Kubernetes cluster both on-premises and in the cloud. We will begin with discussion of the decision process of where to install, on-premises or in the cloud, and what to consider in that process. We will then go through the process of building an on-premises, virtual machine–based Kubernetes cluster using the *kubeadm* installation method. Then next, we will build a cluster in Azure Kubernetes Service. These clusters will be the foundation for all examples in the remainder of the book.

Installation Considerations and Methods

As with pretty much any modern software installation, the first thing you need to decide is: Will you be installing on-premises or to a cloud.

Where to Deploy?

When deploying to a cloud, you need to choose between two major deployment options:

- **Infrastructure as a Service (IaaS):** In an IaaS scenario, you deploy *virtual machines* within your cloud and then install Kubernetes on top of that.

- **Platform as a Service (PaaS):** Kubernetes is also available as a managed service from all the big cloud providers. In a managed service offering, you don't have to worry about any of the underlying infrastructure or redundancy; the cloud provider handles that for you. One thing to consider with PaaS is that you will lose some flexibility in versioning and other features that are available inside Kubernetes as well as the access to the Control Plane Nodes.

© Anthony E. Nocentino, Ben Weissman 2021
A. E. Nocentino and B. Weissman, *SQL Server on Kubernetes*, https://doi.org/10.1007/978-1-4842-7192-6_4

When deploying on-premises, the decision comes down to installing on virtual machines as well or directly on *bare metal*. While there are managed offerings available on-premises as well, those are out of the scope of this book.

The decision between bare metal and virtual machines as your nodes mainly comes down to your anticipated workload. If you're talking about a lot of scalable microservices, Kubernetes Nodes running on VMs will probably give you a lot of extra flexibility. If you're deploying one large single application, the hypervisor in between will require unnecessary overhead. You may be wondering: If you're only running a single application, is Kubernetes even the best platform for this? As so often, the answer is it depends! While it may not be an obvious use case, there are applications like SQL Server Big Data Clusters, which we'll discuss in more depth in Chapter 10. While they often warrant dedicated infrastructure, they only deploy on Kubernetes.

In this book, we will mostly be focusing on an environment using self-managed (on-premises or Infrastructure as a Service) machines using a setup as described in Chapter 1. It doesn't matter if you installed those machines as VMs in the cloud, on-premises, or on bare metal, as Kubernetes abstracts the infrastructure away.

Going forward, looking on where to install a potential production cluster... That question should follow your organization's general strategy. If all you do so far is still on-premises, it might make perfect sense for your Kubernetes cluster to live there as well. If on the other hand you're in the process of migrating or already have migrated major workloads to the cloud, your Kubernetes Cluster probably should follow. In the end, this comes down to your team's skillset and the requirements of your use cases to run on Kubernetes.

Further Considerations

Besides the *where* question, there are of course other considerations about which we'll be talking in more depth over the course of this chapter and the remainder of the book:

- How many Worker Nodes do you need to support your workload?

- What's the CPU and RAM configuration of those nodes?

- Do you need a highly available solution in case the Control Plane fails?

- What is your backup and restore strategy?

- What kind of storage(s) are you going to use?

- How are you going to manage networking between pods and nodes?

While we're at the beginning of your Kubernetes journey, those are all questions that you should have an answer for before considering a rollout of a production system.

Installation Methods

Depending on where you're installing, this will also for the most part determine your installation method. When installing a self-managed cluster, you can choose mainly kubeadm, which is a free way of deploying Kubernetes on *Linux* or enterprise offerings like Red Hat OpenShift. The installation itself is usually triggered through command line tools.

When installing a cloud-based cluster, your cloud provider will take care of the installation part with the exact details behind the scenes being determined by your cloud provider. They usually offer their own command line–based approaches as well as web portals for a guided deployment.

Additional Options

There are a bunch of additional options like using *Docker* Desktop to spin up a Kubernetes Cluster on your laptop or using lightweight hardware like a Raspberry Pi as your deployment target. While they may have valid use cases, especially in non-production environments, we will not go into depth on these in this book.

Also, while there are options to use Windows-based Worker Nodes, we will be focusing on using Linux as our operating system.

We also will not be going through the details of deploying a single-node cluster. If you only have a single *Ubuntu* machine available, you can use the code in Listing 4-1, which will spin up a single-node cluster including *local storage,* but this will not be sufficient for most of the exercises through this book, except for the most basic ones.

Listing 4-1. Install single-node cluster

```
wget -q -O deploy_kubeadm.sh https://bookmark.ws/ArcDemo_Linux
chmod +x deploy_kubeadm.sh
./deploy_kubeadm.sh
```

Installation Requirements

For a self-managed Kubernetes installation, we will be focusing on kubeadm on Linux, more specifically Ubuntu. While CentOS, RHEL, and other Linux distributions are also supported, we just had to decide on one environment, and Ubuntu seems to be the most common choice these days.

The bare minimum system requirements are a system with two CPUs, 2GB on RAM, and swap disabled. This minimum requirement for the Kubernetes components doesn't support any meaningful workloads though. Please make sure that you're using an environment as laid out in Chapter 1. In a production environment, also make sure you have accounted for scalability and redundancy.

In addition to those base system requirements, you'll also need a CRI (Container Runtime Interface) container runtime. As of the time of writing, Kubernetes supports both Docker and *containerd*. As Docker has been deprecated in Kubernetes 1.20 and its support will be removed in Kubernetes version 1.23 or later, we will mainly focus on containerd in this book.

Network Requirements

From a networking perspective, make sure that all machines have unique hostnames, MAC addresses, and IP addresses. Those IP addresses should ideally be on the same subnet, but at the very least must be set up to reach each other.

If you are running a firewall within your network (for the purpose of the labs in this book, we recommend not to run a firewall, simply to avoid running into unnecessary complications with network), Table 4-1 lists all the TCP ports that need to be reachable on the Control Plane.

Table 4-1. Required TCP Ports on Control Plane Node

Component	TCP Port(s)
API	6443
Etcd	2379–2380
Scheduler	10251
Controller Manager	10252
Kubelet	10250

On the nodes, the ports listed in Table 4-2 need to be opened.

Table 4-2. *Required TCP Ports on Worker Nodes*

Component	TCP Port(s)
Kubelet	10250
NodePort	30000–32767

Note   The TCP ports listed here are the default ports. In case you changed those, adjust your firewall rules accordingly.

Getting Kubernetes

Of course, to install Kubernetes, we need to get Kubernetes. The Kubernetes software is maintained on GitHub, so if you go to *https://GitHub.com/Kubernetes/Kubernetes/*, you will find the Kubernetes project. You can also contribute your own ideas and changes to the project. This is also a very valuable resource to understand in detail how things work since you can view the code and learn from other people's experiences with GitHub issues.

In addition to the software itself, this is also where you will find additional documentation.

While in theory you could get the code and compile everything on your own, we'll make our lives a bit easier and install Kubernetes through a package manager.

Building a Self-Managed Cluster

With that theory in place, let's get to work and build our very first Kubernetes Cluster running on Ubuntu machines using kubeadm. We will be using the environment as described in Chapter 1 including the prerequisites mentioned there.

> **Note**   All our scripts are using the hostnames/IP addresses as described in Chapter 1. If you did build your lab using different settings, you will need to adjust those scripts accordingly. For readability purposes, we'll not be pointing out every single instance where this may be required individually.

Getting the VMs Ready

First, we need to get our four VMs (control as well as node-1, node-2, and node-3) ready and install both containerd and the Kubernetes packages. Install and configure them on each of those machines as described in the next two paragraphs. There is no need to install containerd on the storage machine.

Unless mentioned otherwise, just run the commands as stated using a shell on each of the machines. This installation cannot be triggered directly from our administrative workstation.

Installing and Configuring containerd

To install containerd, we need to load two modules (*overlay* and *br_netfilter*) using the code in Listing 4-2. They are needed for the OverlayFS used by the container runtime as well as for networking inside the cluster.

Listing 4-2. Install modprobe overlay and br_netfilter

```
sudo modprobe overlay
sudo modprobe br_netfilter
```

Using the code in Listing 4-3, we need to make sure those are also loaded on reboot.

Listing 4-3. Persist modprobe and br_netfilter

```
cat <<EOF | sudo tee /etc/modules-load.d/containerd.conf
overlay
br_netfilter
EOF
```

containerd also requires a few system parameters, which we can set and persist using the command in Listing 4-4.

Listing 4-4. Persist system parameters for containerd

```
cat <<EOF | sudo tee /etc/sysctl.d/99-kubernetes-cri.conf
net.bridge.bridge-nf-call-iptables  = 1
net.ipv4.ip_forward                 = 1
net.bridge.bridge-nf-call-ip6tables = 1
EOF
```

Next, let's apply those settings without rebooting using the command in Listing 4-5.

Listing 4-5. Apply sysctl changes

```
sudo sysctl --system
```

Now our prerequisites for containerd are in place, so we can install it through *apt-get* as shown in Listing 4-6.

Listing 4-6. Install containerd

```
sudo apt-get update
sudo apt-get install -y containerd
```

containerd requires a configuration file, and we can use containerd itself to generate one with default settings (Listing 4-7).

Listing 4-7. Create containerd config

```
sudo mkdir -p /etc/containerd
sudo containerd config default | sudo tee /etc/containerd/config.toml
```

In this file, we must set the cgroup driver for containerd to system as this is required for the kubelet.

Open the file */etc/containerd/config.toml* in a text editor as root (e.g., through *vi* as shown in Listing 4-8).

Listing 4-8. Edit containerd config

```
sudo vi /etc/containerd/config.toml
```

In this file, find the section shown in Listing 4-9.

Listing 4-9. Section in containerd config

```
[plugins."io.containerd.grpc.v1.cri".containerd.runtimes.runc]
```

Below that, add the two lines shown in Listing 4-10.

Listing 4-10. Lines to be added to containerd config

```
[plugins."io.containerd.grpc.v1.cri".containerd.runtimes.runc.options]
  SystemdCgroup = true
```

Note   Indentation matters here – this can be tabs or spaces! Make sure your file looks like the one in Figure 4-1!

To exit vi and save the file, press *Esc* followed by typing *:x!*.

```
[plugins."io.containerd.grpc.v1.cri".containerd.runtimes]
  [plugins."io.containerd.grpc.v1.cri".containerd.runtimes.runc]
    runtime_type = "io.containerd.runc.v1"
    runtime_engine = ""
    runtime_root = ""
    privileged_without_host_devices = false
    [plugins."io.containerd.grpc.v1.cri".containerd.runtimes.runc.options]
      SystemdCgroup = true
```

Figure 4-1. *Indentation in containerd config file*

Based on our new settings, we can use `systemctl` to restart containerd as shown in Listing 4-11.

Listing 4-11. Restart containerd

```
sudo systemctl restart containerd
```

containerd is now ready for use, and we can move on to the Kubernetes packages. You can confirm the status of the service using the command in Listing 4-12.

Listing 4-12. Status of containerd

```
sudo systemctl status containerd
```

Installing and Configuring Kubernetes Packages

As we will be installing packages from the Google repository, we will need to add Google's apt repository gpg key first (Listing 4-13).

Listing 4-13. Add Google gpg key

```
curl -s https://packages.cloud.google.com/apt/doc/apt-key.gpg | sudo
apt-key add -
```

With that key in place, we can also add the Kubernetes apt repository (Listing 4-14).

Listing 4-14. Add Kubernetes apt repository

```
sudo bash -c 'cat <<EOF >/etc/apt/sources.list.d/kubernetes.list
deb https://apt.kubernetes.io/ kubernetes-xenial main
EOF'
```

Let's update the apt package list and take a look at the available versions for the kubelet using the code in Listing 4-15.

Listing 4-15. Update apt package list

```
sudo apt-get update
apt-cache policy kubelet | head -n 20
```

This shows the available versions, and as you can see in Figure 4-2, at the time of writing, the latest available version is 1.20.4.

```
labuser@control:~$ apt-cache policy kubelet | head -n 20
kubelet:
  Installed: (none)
  Candidate: 1.20.4-00
  Version table:
     1.20.4-00 500
        500 https://apt.kubernetes.io kubernetes-xenial/main amd64 Packages
     1.20.2-00 500
        500 https://apt.kubernetes.io kubernetes-xenial/main amd64 Packages
     1.20.1-00 500
        500 https://apt.kubernetes.io kubernetes-xenial/main amd64 Packages
     1.20.0-00 500
        500 https://apt.kubernetes.io kubernetes-xenial/main amd64 Packages
     1.19.8-00 500
        500 https://apt.kubernetes.io kubernetes-xenial/main amd64 Packages
     1.19.7-00 500
        500 https://apt.kubernetes.io kubernetes-xenial/main amd64 Packages
     1.19.6-00 500
        500 https://apt.kubernetes.io kubernetes-xenial/main amd64 Packages
     1.19.5-00 500
        500 https://apt.kubernetes.io kubernetes-xenial/main amd64 Packages
```

Figure 4-2. *Version list for kubelet*

We can now install *kubelet*, kubeadm, and kubectl as shown in Listing 4-16. If your current machine is also the one you've used to install kubectl in Chapter 1, you may get a message that it's already installed.

Listing 4-16. Install Kubernetes packages

```
sudo apt-get install -y kubelet kubeadm kubectl
```

This will install the latest version of each of these tools. Should you wish to install a previous version, you can specify that as shown in Listing 4-17. The code and samples in this book are not version specific though.

Listing 4-17. Install specific version of Kubernetes packages

```
VERSION=1.20.1-00
sudo apt-get install -y kubelet=$VERSION kubeadm=$VERSION kubectl=$VERSION
```

To avoid automatic updates, we mark those tools (and containerd) as hold (Listing 4-18). This gives us full control over the patching process, running it independent from patching the base operating system.

Listing 4-18. Mark Kubernetes packages and containerd as hold

```
sudo apt-mark hold kubelet kubeadm kubectl containerd
```

Let's check the status of our kubelet and our container runtime (Listing 4-19).

Listing 4-19. Check status of kubelet and containerd

```
sudo systemctl status kubelet.service
sudo systemctl status containerd.service
```

As you can see in Figure 4-3, the kubelet will enter a crashloop. This is normal behavior until a cluster is created or the node is joined to an existing cluster (you can leave that process by pressing *q*).

```
labuser@control:~$ sudo systemctl status kubelet.service
● kubelet.service - kubelet: The Kubernetes Node Agent
   Loaded: loaded (/lib/systemd/system/kubelet.service; enabled; vendor preset: enabled)
  Drop-In: └─10-kubeadm.conf
   Active: activating (auto-restart) (Result: exit-code) since Mon 2021-03-01 10:03:15 UTC; 5s ago
     Docs: https://kubernetes.io/docs/home/
  Process: 3997 ExecStart=/usr/bin/kubelet $KUBELET_KUBECONFIG_ARGS $KUBELET_CONFIG_ARGS $KUBELET_KUBEADM_ARGS $KUBELET_EXTRA_ARGS (code=exited, status=255)
 Main PID: 3997 (code=exited, status=255)

Mar 01 10:03:15 control systemd[1]: kubelet.service: Main process exited, code=exited, status=255/n/a
Mar 01 10:03:15 control systemd[1]: kubelet.service: Failed with result 'exit-code'.
```

Figure 4-3. *Status of kubelet and containerd*

Also make sure that both services are set to start when the system starts up. This can be set through the commands in Listing 4-20.

Listing 4-20. Enable startup on reboot for kubelet and containerd

```
sudo systemctl enable kubelet.service
sudo systemctl enable containerd.service
```

Note   Remember to repeat this process and install and configure these packages on *control*, *node1*, *node2*, and *node3* individually!

Creating a Control Plane

With our container runtime and Kubernetes packages now in place, we can move on to create our Control Plane.

Note   All commands in this section need to be executed on your *control VM*.

We start by generating a configuration file as shown in Listing 4-21.

Listing 4-21. Create kubeadm configuration file

```
kubeadm config print init-defaults | tee ClusterConfiguration.yaml
```

Inside the default Cluster configuration file, we need to change a couple of things. Some of them can be done in an automated way as shown in Listing 4-22. This will

- **Set** the IP endpoint for the API Server localAPIEndpoint. advertiseAddress to the IP address of our Control Plane Node.

- **Change** the nodeRegistration.criSocket from Docker to containerd. In a future release of Kubernetes, this will become the default.

- **Set** the cgroup driver for the kubelet to system, which is not yet defined in this file, as the default is cgroupfs.

- **Define** the podNetwork.

Listing 4-22. Modify kubeadm config file

```
sed -i 's/ advertiseAddress: 1.2.3.4/ advertiseAddress: 172.16.94.10/'
ClusterConfiguration.yaml

sed -i 's/ criSocket: \/var\/run\/dockershim\.sock/ criSocket: \/run\/
containerd\/containerd\.sock/' ClusterConfiguration.yaml

cat <<EOF | cat >> ClusterConfiguration.yaml
---
apiVersion: kubelet.config.k8s.io/v1beta1
kind: KubeletConfiguration
cgroupDriver: systemd
EOF
```

We also need to edit the *kubernetesVersion* in this file to match the version you installed earlier. First, confirm the installed version using the command in Listing 4-23.

Listing 4-23. Get current kubeadm version

```
kubeadm version
```

As you can see in Figure 4-4, we have version 1.20.4 installed – unless you went with another version.

```
labuser@control:~$ kubeadm version
kubeadm version: &version.Info{Major:"1", Minor:"20", GitVersion:"v1.20.4", GitCo
mmit:"e87da0bd6e03ec3fea7933c4b5263d15laafd07c", GitTreeState:"clean", BuildDate:
"2021-02-18T16:09:38Z", GoVersion:"gol.15.8", Compiler:"gc", Platform:"linux/amd6
4"}
```

Figure 4-4. *Current version of kubeadm installed*

With this information, we can now edit the file (e.g., through *vi)* *ClusterConfiguration.yaml* and make sure the version matches as shown in Figure 4-5.

```
imageRepository: k8s.gcr.io
kind: ClusterConfiguration
kubernetesVersion: v1.20.4
```

Figure 4-5. *Set current version of kubelet in ClusterConfiguration.yaml.*

In the *networking* section, add a line that sets the *podSubnet* to *10.244.0.10/16* as shown in Figure 4-6, which is required by the flannel network plugin.

```
networking:
  dnsDomain: cluster.local
  serviceSubnet: 10.96.0.0/12
  podSubnet: 10.244.0.0/16
```

Figure 4-6. *podSubnet in ClusterConfiguration.yaml*

Now, we're ready to initialize our cluster using kubeadm as shown in Listing 4-24.

Listing 4-24. Initialize cluster

```
sudo kubeadm init \
    --config=ClusterConfiguration.yaml \
    --cri-socket /run/containerd/containerd.sock
```

This will take a few minutes and will output its progress constantly. The result should look similar to what you see in Figure 4-7.

```
Your Kubernetes control-plane has initialized successfully!

To start using your cluster, you need to run the following as a regular user:

  mkdir -p $HOME/.kube
  sudo cp -i /etc/kubernetes/admin.conf $HOME/.kube/config
  sudo chown $(id -u):$(id -g) $HOME/.kube/config

Alternatively, if you are the root user, you can run:

  export KUBECONFIG=/etc/kubernetes/admin.conf

You should now deploy a pod network to the cluster.
Run "kubectl apply -f [podnetwork].yaml" with one of the options listed at:
  https://kubernetes.io/docs/concepts/cluster-administration/addons/

Then you can join any number of worker nodes by running the following on each as root:

kubeadm join 172.16.94.10:6443 --token abcdef.0123456789abcdef \
    --discovery-token-ca-cert-hash sha256:9c86ee0fa239734c75f8c7233bdd628424098bfd451e154d6280fdf499a69c52
```

Figure 4-7. *Output of kubeadm init*

To make sure that we can interact with our cluster on a non-elevated shell as well, we need to create a config file and store it in our home directory as shown in Listing 4-25.

Listing 4-25. Create kubectl configuration

```
mkdir -p $HOME/.kube
sudo cp -i /etc/kubernetes/admin.conf $HOME/.kube/config
sudo chown $(id -u):$(id -g) $HOME/.kube/config
```

Note   If you are using an administrative workstation, you can take this file and copy it or its contents to *.kube/config* in your home directory on this workstation. This will allow you to communicate with your cluster from that workstation.

Pod Networking

Before we can join our Worker Nodes, we need to ensure that our Pod Network is set up. There are many different solutions out there, and we have decided to keep it simple and use *flannel*. While it doesn't have all the advanced configuration settings like *Calico*, another version popular for Pod Networking, it works without any additional configuration on local and cloud networks, which tend to restrict *IPIP* packages, for example.

Download the default manifest using the *wget* command in Listing 4-26.

Listing 4-26. Download flannel

```
wget https://raw.githubusercontent.com/flannel-io/flannel/master/
Documentation/kube-flannel.yml
```

If you want, you can look at the file first, but there are no required changes, so we'll go straight ahead and install it using kubectl (Listing 4-27). We will be talking more about kubectl in the next chapter, so don't worry if this feels a bit unexplained at this point.

Listing 4-27. Install flannel

```
kubectl apply -f kube-flannel.yml
```

Your Pod Networking with flannel is now set up.

Storage

While it would typically be configured at this stage, we will be deploying our cluster without any attached storage at first. As Kubernetes separates compute and data, this is totally doable. Our first exercises on interacting with our cluster in the next chapter won't require any storage. We will be handling storage concepts in Kubernetes in depth in Chapter 6 before deploying SQL Server – which does require storage.

Adding Nodes to a Cluster

Our Control Plane is ready, but we're not quite ready to join our nodes yet. For a node to be able to join a cluster, we need a token. The easiest way is to directly generate a *join command* using kubeadm as shown in Listing 4-28.

Listing 4-28. Generate token and join command

```
kubeadm token create --print-join-command
```

The output looks similar to what you see in Figure 4-8.

```
labuser@control:~$ kubeadm token create --print-join-command
kubeadm join 172.16.94.10:6443 --token pdru87.9yjxcif8n4bb4yp0    --discovery-token-ca-cert-hash sha256:9c86ee0fa239734c75f8c7233bdd628424098bfd451e154d6280fdf499a69c52
```

Figure 4-8. *Join command (generated on Control Plane Node)*

> **Note**   Depending on your installed version, you may get a warning that Docker is not your container runtime. It is safe to ignore this warning.

Now, we can take this command and run it (as root; see Listing 4-29) on each of our desired Worker Nodes, which will then initiate the join process. Your individual join command will be different because the CA certificate is unique. The join token is a ticket valid for 24 hours, so if you want to add more nodes later, you will need to create a new token.

Listing 4-29. kubeadm join command

```
sudo kubeadm join 172.16.94.10:6443 \
        --token pdru87.9yjxcif8n4bb4yp0  \
        --discovery-token-ca-cert-hash sha256:9c86ee0fa239734c75f8c7233bdd
            628424098bfd451e154d6280fdf499a69c52
```

> **Note**   Make sure to add *sudo* – the command needs to be run as root, and the *--print-join-command* does not add it for you!

The nodes will report that they have started the join process as you can see in Figure 4-9.

```
labuser@node1:~$ sudo kubeadm join 172.16.94.10:6443 --token pdru87.9yjxcif8n4bb4yp0  --discovery-token-ca-cert
[preflight] Running pre-flight checks
[preflight] Reading configuration from the cluster...
[preflight] FYI: You can look at this config file with 'kubectl -n kube-system get cm kubeadm-config -o yaml'
[kubelet-start] Writing kubelet configuration to file "/var/lib/kubelet/config.yaml"
[kubelet-start] Writing kubelet environment file with flags to file "/var/lib/kubelet/kubeadm-flags.env"
[kubelet-start] Starting the kubelet
[kubelet-start] Waiting for the kubelet to perform the TLS Bootstrap...

This node has joined the cluster:
* Certificate signing request was sent to apiserver and a response was received.
* The Kubelet was informed of the new secure connection details.

Run 'kubectl get nodes' on the control-plane to see this node join the cluster.
```

Figure 4-9. *Join command (executed on Worker Node)*

Let us list the nodes by running kubectl on the Control Plane (see Listing 4-30).

Listing 4-30. List nodes in cluster

```
kubectl get nodes
```

We will see that the nodes are showing up but are *NotReady* yet (see Figure 4-10).

```
labuser@control:~$ kubectl get nodes
NAME       STATUS     ROLES                   AGE       VERSION
control    Ready      control-plane,master    7m33s     v1.20.4
node1      NotReady   <none>                   27s       v1.20.4
```

Figure 4-10. *Nodes in cluster*

If you run the command again after a few minutes, the nodes will all show as *Ready*. Nodes will show as *NotReady* because the pods that run Pod Networking and kube-proxy are being deployed. You should not proceed working on that cluster until all your nodes show as Ready, as in Figure 4-11.

```
labuser@control:~$ kubectl get nodes
NAME       STATUS     ROLES                   AGE       VERSION
control    Ready      control-plane,master    2m27s     v1.20.4
node1      Ready      <none>                   74s       v1.20.4
node2      Ready      <none>                   68s       v1.20.4
node3      Ready      <none>                   64s       v1.20.4
```

Figure 4-11. *All Nodes in Cluster showing Ready*

Building a Cluster in the Cloud with Azure Kubernetes Service

With our self-managed cluster in place, let's also install a managed Kubernetes cluster in Azure using Azure Kubernetes Service.

Note   This exercise can also be executed from your administrative workstation. It could also be achieved through Azure Portal.

We will be using the *Azure CLI* again for this exercise.

Unless you are still logged in from the session in Chapter 1, let's start by logging in to your Azure account and setting the subscription to be used as shown in Listing 4-31.

Listing 4-31. Log in to Azure account

```
az login
az account set -s <YourSubscription>
```

Next, let's create a dedicated resource group as shown in Listing 4-32. Modify the name and location to fit your needs.

Listing 4-32. Create resource group

```
az group create --name "Kubernetes-Cloud" --location eastus
```

We're already ready to go to create our cluster. We will be using the code in Listing 4-33, which will be creating a three-node cluster named AKSCluster in our previously generated resource group.

Listing 4-33. Create AKS cluster (bash)

```
az aks create \
    --resource-group "Kubernetes-Cloud" \
    --generate-ssh-keys \
    --name AKSCluster \
    --node-count 3
```

In case you are running this command from PowerShell, make sure to modify the line breaks as shown in Listing 4-34. This applies to any multi-line listing in this book.

Listing 4-34. Create AKS cluster (PowerShell)

```
az aks create `
    --resource-group "Kubernetes-Cloud" `
    --generate-ssh-keys `
    --name AKSCluster `
    --node-count 3
```

Once the cluster creation has finished, the CLI will report back as shown in Figure 4-12.

```
labuser@control:~$ az aks create     --resource-group "Kubernetes-Cloud"     --generate-ssh-keys     --name AKSCluster     --node-count 3
{
  "agentPoolProfiles": [
    {
      "count": 3,
      "dnsPrefix": null,
      "fqdn": null,
      "name": "nodepool1",
      "osDiskSizeGb": 128,
      "osType": "Linux",
      "ports": null,
      "storageProfile": "ManagedDisks",
      "vmSize": "Standard_D1_v2",
      "vnetSubnetId": null
    }
  ],
  "dnsPrefix": "AKSCluster-Kubernetes-Cloud-92cc49",
  "fqdn": "akscluster-kubernetes-cloud-92cc49-0cb3a695.hcp.eastus.azmk8s.io",
  "id": "/subscriptions/                              /resourcegroups/Kubernetes-Cloud/providers/Microsoft.ContainerService/managedC
  "kubernetesVersion": "1.20.2",
  "linuxProfile": {
    "adminUsername": "azureuser",
    "ssh": {
      "publicKeys": [
        {
          "keyData": "ssh-rsa AAAAB3NzaC1yc2EAAAADAQABAAAABAQC2zCru1QrcykUMtM/NUwEndgT/c0zkLCsOKkBq9AP434EoYN6qWENPoalwGgrZIIgKMmnrEnMH1Uzr
iY42ysjIGnnbYkGksALpP3Lif7hdPPLvwsD2DtNQkW416FXOHEPUHOVqVxIst7UIKOiqdW8k7Gru0jEmI2FPs/kUWx1nV6ikYU2InPi2KEZepdsKWzwCWet1gABZ7Ad76PxJnAC69C
        }
      ]
    }
  },
  "location": "eastus",
  "name": "AKSCluster",
  "provisioningState": "Succeeded",
  "resourceGroup": "Kubernetes-Cloud",
  "servicePrincipalProfile": {
    "clientId": "6a066171-c5c9-4800-ad04-134ab102ec3b",
    "keyVaultSecretRef": null,
    "secret": null
  },
  "tags": null,
  "type": "Microsoft.ContainerService/ManagedClusters"
}
```

Figure 4-12. *Output of az aks create*

For more options when creating an AKS cluster (like machine size), please refer to the official docs at *https://docs.microsoft.com/en-us/cli/azure/aks?view=azure-cli-latest#az_aks_create*.

To be able to communicate with our cluster, we need to add its credentials and merge them to our existing configuration file. Run the command in Listing 4-35 to do that. This will allow us to connect to this system remotely using certificate-based user authentication.

Listing 4-35. Retrieve credentials for AKS cluster

```
az aks get-credentials --resource-group "Kubernetes-Cloud" --name
AKSCluster
```

We now have two clusters configured and their credentials stored in our kubectl configuration. We will explain in the next chapter how we can use kubectl to communicate with and switch between those clusters.

Note   While the tools and syntax may differ, the general process is the same to deploying other managed Kubernetes cluster solutions like GKE or EKS. Get their tools, deploy the cluster, and download the cluster credentials.

Summary

In this chapter, we looked at some installation considerations and what you need to know before you install Kubernetes. We also covered the how with regard to installing Kubernetes, both self-managed on Linux and through a managed cloud service. In the next chapter, we will look at how we can interact with our cluster through kubectl.

CHAPTER 5

Interacting with Your Kubernetes Cluster

With a functioning cluster up and running, we will now learn the core way to interact with our cluster, *kubectl*. Kubectl is the command line client used to deploy and maintain applications in Kubernetes as well as to administrate the cluster itself. With kubectl preliminaries behind us, we will learn how to deploy and access applications in our cluster.

To make sure that your cluster can be reached from the administrative workstation, copy the kubectl configuration to it using the command in Listing 5-1.

Listing 5-1. Copy kubectl config to Windows workstation

```
mkdir c:\users\labuser\.kube

$LinuxPW="Str@ngPassw0rd"

pscp -P 22 -pw $LinuxPW labuser@control:/home/labuser/.kube/config
c:\users\labuser\.kube
```

Using kubectl to Interact with Your Cluster

Kubectl is a command line tool to create, read, update, or delete pretty much any kind of resource in Kubernetes. Now remember, in Kubernetes, everything goes through the API Server, and so kubectl is your primary way to interact with the API Server. Any time you need to create, modify, or query something in Kubernetes, this is the primary CLI tool for doing that.

© Anthony E. Nocentino, Ben Weissman 2021
A. E. Nocentino and B. Weissman, *SQL Server on Kubernetes*, https://doi.org/10.1007/978-1-4842-7192-6_5

Most kubectl commands effectively consist of three parts:

- **Operations:** What do you want to do?

- **Resources:** What do you want to do it to?

- **Output:** For commands that produce an output, how should the output be formatted?

A typical command would look like the generic example in Listing 5-2.

Listing 5-2. Generic kubectl command

```
kubectl <operation> <resource type> <resource name> <output options>
```

The command from Listing 5-3, for example, will return a detailed list of all the nodes in our cluster.

Listing 5-3. Kubectl command to retrieve detailed list of nodes in a cluster

```
kubectl get nodes -o wide
```

The output from this command should look similar to what we see in Figure 5-1.

```
labuser@control:~$ kubectl get nodes -o wide
NAME      STATUS   ROLES                  AGE     VERSION   INTERNAL-IP    EXTERNAL-IP   OS-IMAGE          KERNEL-VERSION    CONTAINER-RUNTIME
control   Ready    control-plane,master   4m21s   v1.20.1   172.16.94.10   <none>        Ubuntu 18.04.5 LTS   5.4.0-1039-azure   docker://19.3.6
node1     Ready    <none>                 71s     v1.20.1   172.16.94.11   <none>        Ubuntu 18.04.5 LTS   5.4.0-1039-azure   docker://19.3.6
node2     Ready    <none>                 81s     v1.20.1   172.16.94.12   <none>        Ubuntu 18.04.5 LTS   5.4.0-1039-azure   docker://19.3.6
node3     Ready    <none>                 77s     v1.20.1   172.16.94.13   <none>        Ubuntu 18.04.5 LTS   5.4.0-1039-azure   docker://19.3.6
labuser@control:~$ []
```

Figure 5-1. *Output of kubectl get node -o wide*

If you are looking for a resource from a specific namespace, this filter would also be passed on to kubectl. The command in Listing 5-4 would return all the pods running in the mssql-server namespace.

Listing 5-4. Kubectl command to retrieve pods in a namespace

```
kubectl get pods -n kube-system
```

Note   Like most tools in the Kubernetes ecosystem, kubectl runs cross-platform, so these commands are identical no matter if you run them on Windows, Linux, or a Mac.

One of the exceptions to this syntax is shown in Listing 5-5.

Listing 5-5. Kubectl command to get a general overview of your cluster

```
kubectl cluster-info
```

This command doesn't specify an operation, resource, or output. Those aren't needed as this command gives us a general overview of our cluster like its Control Plane IP address and port as well as the status of KubeDNS.

You should receive an output that more or less matches the one in Figure 5-2.

```
labuser@control:~$ kubectl cluster-info
Kubernetes control plane is running at https://172.16.94.10:6443
KubeDNS is running at https://172.16.94.10:6443/api/v1/namespaces/kube-system/services/kube-dns:dns/proxy

To further debug and diagnose cluster problems, use 'kubectl cluster-info dump'.
labuser@control:~$ 
```

Figure 5-2. *Output of kubectl cluster-info*

Let us take a closer look at the different parts of a kubectl command.

Operations

There are a ton of operations in Kubernetes using kubectl, so let's focus on the core ones and look at them in more detail:

- **Apply:** This will deploy the content of a file – typically a YAML file – to your Kubernetes cluster. We used this during our cluster's deployment in the previous chapter, for example, when we added flannel. Apply will also be used for any declarative deployment of applications into your cluster.

- **Create:** Create allows you to imperatively add resources to your cluster, and we'll take a deeper look at this later in this chapter when we'll explain how to deploy an application to your cluster. In many cases, create and apply can both be used with the same result.

- **Run:** Run will allow you to start a pod and specify the container image, basically bootstrapping the most basic pod configuration.

- **Explain:** This gives you the documentation for a particular Kubernetes API Object or resource, listing the description and the fields needed to construct that object. This is especially useful when building manifests and can also be used to quickly find field names for objects.

- **Delete:** This will delete a specified resource.

- **Get:** What kubectl get will do is display the basic information about the specified resource type.

- **Describe:** Describe gives you detailed resource information, and this is used to display very detailed information about a particular resource. This is your first stop when things go wrong: the events section at the bottom is a great place for troubleshooting.

- **Exec:** Exec allows you to exec a command inside a container in a pod.

- **Logs:** This allows you to view the logs from a container running inside of a pod.

As mentioned before, this is a short list of the – in our opinion – most critical ones, just to get you started. You will find a full list at *https://kubernetes.io/docs/reference/kubectl/overview/#operations*, and we strongly encourage you to check those out!

Resources

When working at the command line, we're going to combine kubectl with an operation like the ones that we saw earlier with a resource. Basically, *what* do you want to perform that operation against. We've also introduced things like nodes and pods and services, and honestly, there are many, many more objects available inside of Kubernetes that we can work with. That's how we go ahead and specify what type of resource we want to perform the operation against.

Some of the most common resource types would be

- Nodes (no)

- Pods (po)

- Services (svc)

Now here you can see in parentheses an alias to represent that particular type of resource, so nodes no, pods po, and services svc, and that's a good way so that we can get real quick at the command line executing these commands.

They are completely synonymous when using kubectl, so running the commands in Listing 5-6 will get you the exact same result twice.

Listing 5-6. Kubectl command with and without resource type alias

```
kubectl get no
kubectl get nodes
```

The official documentation at *https://kubernetes.io/docs/reference/kubectl/ overview/#resource-types* has the full list of resource types available for you!

By the way, you can also get a list of all the available resource types in your Kubernetes cluster by running the command in Listing 5-7. This is also another example for a command that doesn't use operations, resources, or output options.

Listing 5-7. Kubectl command to list available resource types

```
kubectl api-resources
```

Output

The final part of a kubectl command construct is modifying its output. We can specify kubectl's output format by adding additional flags to our commands.

One very helpful format that we want to introduce you to is *wide*, which will add additional information about our Kubernetes objects that are working with standard out.

We can also output our Kubernetes objects as *YAML* and *JSON*. YAML- and JSON-formatted files are at the core of how Kubernetes describes things declaratively, giving us the ability to describe our configurations in code. We can use kubectl to output YAML or JSON, and this is a very valuable way to get configuration data out of our cluster and describe the resources that we've deployed in our cluster. We can persist this to file and exchange it with other systems, other environments, and other developers if we need to.

Another option is *jsonpath*, which will only get you a specific subset or value from your JSON output. This is especially useful when you want to retrieve values like ports or IP addresses, for example, to be subsequently used in variables in a script.

The full list of output options can be found at *https://kubernetes.io/docs/ reference/kubectl/overview/#output-options*. Another very helpful resource, especially when you're still getting acquainted with kubectl, is the kubectl cheatsheet: *https://kubernetes.io/docs/reference/kubectl/cheatsheet/*.

Kubectl Context

Kubectl can be used to manage multiple Kubernetes clusters from the same workstation. This is handled through so-called contexts. A context is the combination of a cluster and credentials to be used to log into that cluster.

Let's begin by listing all the contexts that are currently available to us using the command in Listing 5-8.

Listing 5-8. Show config of kubectl including all contexts

```
kubectl config view
```

As we can see in Figure 5-3, we have our kubernetes-admin context (which is our kubeadm cluster) and the AKSCluster context (which is our cluster in Azure Kubernetes Service).

```
labuser@control:~$ kubectl config view
apiVersion: v1
clusters:
- cluster:
    certificate-authority-data: DATA+OMITTED
    server: https://akscluster-kubernetes-cloud-92cc49-0cb3a695.hcp.eastus.azmk8s.io:443
  name: AKSCluster
- cluster:
    certificate-authority-data: DATA+OMITTED
    server: https://172.16.94.10:6443
  name: kubernetes
contexts:
- context:
    cluster: AKSCluster
    user: clusterUser_Kubernetes-Cloud_AKSCluster
  name: AKSCluster
- context:
    cluster: kubernetes
    user: kubernetes-admin
  name: kubernetes-admin@kubernetes
current-context: AKSCluster
kind: Config
preferences: {}
users:
- name: clusterUser_Kubernetes-Cloud_AKSCluster
  user:
    client-certificate-data: REDACTED
    client-key-data: REDACTED
    token: REDACTED
- name: kubernetes-admin
  user:
    client-certificate-data: REDACTED
    client-key-data: REDACTED
```

Figure 5-3. *View of current kubectl config*

Next, let's check which context we're currently using by running the command in Listing 5-9.

Listing 5-9. Get current kubectl context

```
kubectl config current-context
```

As shown in Figure 5-4, our current context is kubernetes-admin, so any kubectl command at this point will be executed against our kubeadm cluster.

```
labuser@control:~$ kubectl config current-context
kubernetes-admin@kubernetes
labuser@control:~$ █
```

Figure 5-4. *Current kubectl context*

Let's change the context to AKSCluster using Listing 5-10.

Listing 5-10. Switch kubectl context to AKSCluster

```
kubectl config use-context AKSCluster
```

This will change our current context to aks-admin. All commands in kubectl will now be executed against the AKS cluster.

Note   Unless stated otherwise, all exercises in this and the upcoming chapters should be executed in the context *kubernetes-admin@kubernetes*.

Application Deployment in Kubernetes

So now that we know how to interact with our cluster at the command line, let's move the conversation to application deployment in Kubernetes.

Like most commands in Kubernetes being executed through kubectl, applications can be deployed using either an imperative or a declarative configuration.

Imperative Deployments

When you're using imperative configuration, you're generally going to be executing commands at the command line one at a time, and you're going to be operating on one object at a time.

Let's run the command in Listing 5-11.

Listing 5-11. Kubectl command to create a deployment using nginx

```
kubectl create deployment nginx --image=nginx
```

The command is sent to the API Server, which will create a deployment named nginx based on the nginx image, but we're only operating on one object at a time on the command line.

This also works with other types of objects of course. The command in Listing 5-12, for example, will again use the nginx image, but it will create a single pod running it.

Listing 5-12. Kubectl command to run a new nginx pod

```
kubectl run nginx --image=nginx
```

While this is certainly a straightforward way to manage a system, if your application stack starts to grow and your configurations and your deployments become more complex, managing each individual object at the command line isn't really a sustainable way to manage or maintain your system. We're going to want to do things declaratively, and this is a core principle behind Kubernetes where we define the desired state of our application or the cluster itself in code using YAML or JSON.

Let us look at the pods using the command in Listing 5-13.

Listing 5-13. kubectl command to list pods

```
kubectl get pods
```

We will see (Figure 5-5) both our pods: the one that we spun up individually (named nginx) and the one from our deployment (named nginx-6799fc88d8-fj928). The name of the pod from our deployment is random and will change every single time the pod gets terminated and a new pod from the same deployment is created.

```
labuser@control:~$ kubectl get pods
NAME                        READY   STATUS             RESTARTS   AGE
nginx                       0/1     ContainerCreating  0          17s
nginx-6799fc88d8-fj928      0/1     ContainerCreating  0          44s
labuser@control:~$ []
```

Figure 5-5. *Output of kubectl get pods*

Before we move on to declarative deployments though, let's clean up and delete the previously created deployment and pod using the command in Listing 5-14.

Listing 5-14. Kubectl command to remove the imperatively created resources

```
kubectl delete deployment nginx
kubectl delete pod nginx
```

The deletion of the deployment will complete immediately, whereas the deletion of the individual pod will only return once the pod has been terminated and deleted.

Declarative Deployments

For either more complex scenarios or simply the advantage of an easier way to deploy the same configuration of an object to another cluster – for example, when pushing an application from a development to a test system – it is therefore highly recommended to use a manifest-based declarative approach. Your manifests should also go to your source control system just like any other code you're using in your environment. In this case, we will just use a manifest that can be written in JSON or YAML and feed it to the API Server using a command like the one in Listing 5-15. By the way, manifests written in YAML will be converted to JSON by Kubernetes.

Listing 5-15. Kubectl command to feed a YAML file to the API Server

```
kubectl apply -f deployment.yaml
```

This command would take the contents of the deployment.yaml file and pass them to the API Server for Kubernetes to create the resources defined in the manifest.

A manifest can consist of many different object types, so we could have a YAML that first creates a storage class followed by a persisted volume and volume claim followed by a deployment and a service definition, for example. All in the same file. All deployed through one single command on the command line.

As also mentioned earlier, we can use kubectl to generate those manifests using the output. Let's start by generating a manifest for a deployment matching the one we've previously created imperatively using the code in Listing 5-16. To do so, we add an output format and the dry-run switch, which will only generate the manifest but won't deploy anything to our cluster.

Listing 5-16. Kubectl command to generate YAML manifest for nginx deployment

```
kubectl create deployment nginx --image=nginx --dry-run=client -o yaml
```

The output can be found in Listing 5-17.

Listing 5-17. Manifest generated from previous listing

```
apiVersion: apps/v1
kind: Deployment
metadata:
  creationTimestamp: null
  labels:
    app: nginx
  name: nginx
spec:
  replicas: 1
  selector:
    matchLabels:
      app: nginx
  strategy: {}
  template:
    metadata:
      creationTimestamp: null
      labels:
        app: nginx
    spec:
      containers:
      - image: nginx
        name: nginx
        resources: {}
```

Let's generate that manifest again, but this time, we will redirect the output to a file called nginx.yaml as shown in Listing 5-18.

Listing 5-18. Kubectl command to generate YAML manifest for nginx deployment redirected to a file

```
kubectl create deployment nginx --image=nginx --dry-run=client -o yaml >
nginx.yaml
```

We can now take that file and create a deployment declaratively. Do this using the command in Listing 5-19.

Listing 5-19. Declarative deployment using the previously generated manifest

```
kubectl apply -f nginx.yaml
```

This will generate a deployment like the previous one. By running the command in Listing 5-20, we can verify that our one replica (as defined in the manifest) is ready.

Listing 5-20. Check the status of this deployment

```
kubectl get deployment nginx
```

The output, as shown in Figure 5-6, will confirm the status of our deployment.

```
NAME      READY    UP-TO-DATE    AVAILABLE    AGE
nginx     1/1      1             1            15m
```

Figure 5-6. *Output of kubectl get deployment nginx*

Modifying a Deployment

Of course, an existing deployment can also be modified without a full redeployment.

Let's assume, for example, you want to update the number of replicas – or Pods – in the existing deployment.

At first sight, the easiest way seems to be, again, to do this imperatively as shown in Listing 5-21.

Listing 5-21. Scale up nginx deployment to two replicas

```
kubectl scale deployment nginx --replicas=2
```

As you can see in Figure 5-7, the deployment is now showing two replicas.

```
NAME      READY    UP-TO-DATE    AVAILABLE    AGE
nginx     2/2      2             2            6m3s
```

Figure 5-7. *Output of kubectl get deployment nginx after rescaling to two replicas*

But now, our manifest file and our deployment are out of sync, as the manifest still reflects only one replica.

A better way would be to edit the manifest using a text editor. Open the file in a text editor of your choice and replace the original replica definition as shown in Listing 5-22 with the new definition of 20 replicas as shown in Listing 5-23.

Listing 5-22. Existing replica definition with one replica

```
spec:
  replicas: 1
```

Listing 5-23. New replica definition with 20 replicas

```
spec:
  replicas: 20
```

Now, we can reapply the manifest (see Listing 5-24), which will scale up our deployment to 20 replicas.

Listing 5-24. Applying the new definition using kubectl

```
kubectl apply -f nginx.yaml
```

As you can see in Figure 5-8, the deployment is now showing 20 replicas (note that it will take some time for all of those replicas to show as ready).

NAME	READY	UP-TO-DATE	AVAILABLE	AGE
nginx	4/20	20	4	35m

Figure 5-8. *Output of kubectl get deployment nginx after rescaling to 20 replicas*

A third way to modify an existing object is *kubectl edit*. While this also comes with the disadvantage of losing sync between your YAML file and what's actually deployed on your cluster, this is a very handy way of making multiple changes to a deployment, for example, at once.

Run the code in Listing 5-25.

Listing 5-25. Edit a running deployment

```
kubectl edit deployment nginx
```

This will open the full manifest of the current deployment in your default text editor. Find the line with the previously defined 20 replicas and change it to 30. When closing and saving this editor, those changes will immediately be applied, which we can check again using kubectl get deployment. The result is also shown in Figure 5-9.

```
NAME     READY    UP-TO-DATE    AVAILABLE    AGE
nginx    30/30    30            30           42m
```

Figure 5-9. *Output of kubectl get deployment nginx after rescaling to 30 replicas*

Exposing and Accessing Services in Your Cluster

Now, we have a scaled deployment of nginx, but the applications running in the pods are not yet accessible. Let's keep moving forward and expose that deployment as a Kubernetes service with a persistent IP address and port for our application to run on.

A service can be created using *kubectl expose.*

Exposing a Service of Type ClusterIP

If you run the code in Listing 5-26, this will create a service that is exposed on port 80, also targeting port 80 (as that's the default for nginx).

Listing 5-26. Expose nginx deployment as a ClusterIP service

```
kubectl expose deployment nginx --port=80 --target-port=80
```

The port defines the port the service is listening on, whereas the target port is the port the application is listening on inside the container. As we did not provide any other options, the type of that service will be ClusterIP, which is the default service type. We can see that by running the command in Listing 5-27.

Listing 5-27. Get service details

```
kubectl get service nginx
```

As you can see in Figure 5-10, this also shows the IP address that this service is running on.

```
labuser@control:~$ kubectl get service nginx
NAME     TYPE         CLUSTER-IP        EXTERNAL-IP    PORT(S)    AGE
nginx    ClusterIP    10.109.180.180    <none>         80/TCP     5s
labuser@control:~$ ▌
```

Figure 5-10. *Output of kubectl get service nginx*

While all these commands are imperative – which is, as we've mentioned before, fine for testing, but YAML manifests should be used in general – you can also just modify the command by adding the dry-run switch to generate a YAML manifest, which you can then apply to your cluster as shown in Listing 5-28.

Listing 5-28. Create manifest to expose nginx deployment as a ClusterIP service

```
kubectl expose deployment nginx --port=80 --target-port=80
--dry-run=client -o yaml
```

By the way, if you only want to retrieve the ClusterIP, this is a perfect use case for the output format jsonpath as shown in Listing 5-29. This is especially helpful when storing this value in a variable in an automation script.

Listing 5-29. Retrieve only the ClusterIP through kubectl

```
kubectl get service nginx -o jsonpath='{ .spec.clusterIP }'
```

We could now access this service, for example, by running the *curl* request in Listing 5-30 (make sure to change the IP address to the ClusterIP of the service in your cluster).

Listing 5-30. Access ClusterIP service

```
curl http://10.109.180.180/
```

As we've elaborated in Chapter 3, a ClusterIP service can be reached from any node and pod within your cluster but not from the outside. Depending on your application scenario, this may be sufficient or not. Let's assume you want to make sure that your service is reachable from outside the cluster.

First, delete the existing service using the command in Listing 5-31.

Listing 5-31. Delete nginx service

```
kubectl delete service nginx
```

Exposing a Service of Type NodePort

If you want to expose a service so it can also be accessed from machines that are not part of your Kubernetes cluster, we need to expose this service as type NodePort.

To do so, we simply add the type switch as shown in Listing 5-32.

Listing 5-32. Expose nginx deployment as a NodePort service

```
kubectl expose deployment nginx --port=80 --target-port=80 --type=NodePort
```

Let's take a look at this service using the command in Listing 5-33.

Listing 5-33. Get service details

```
kubectl get service nginx
```

As you can see in Figure 5-11, the service is now showing type NodePort and also the (dynamic) port that our service has been deployed with.

```
labuser@control:~$ kubectl get service nginx
NAME     TYPE       CLUSTER-IP      EXTERNAL-IP    PORT(S)        AGE
nginx    NodePort   10.102.55.255   <none>         80:31260/TCP   9s
labuser@control:~$ ▮
```

Figure 5-11. *Output of kubectl get service nginx*

This port will not change for the lifetime of the service. If you delete and expose it again though, it will most probably show a different port.

Just like with the ClusterIP in the previous example, we can use jsonpath to retrieve only the NodePort as shown in Listing 5-34.

Listing 5-34. Retrieve only the nodePort through kubectl

```
kubectl get service nginx -o jsonpath='{ .spec.ports[*].nodePort }'
```

A service of type NodePort can be accessed on any of the Kubernetes cluster's nodes. In our example, the requests shown in Listing 5-35 may all end up on different replicas of our deployment but will all result in the same output.

Listing 5-35. Access NodePort service

```
curl http://control:31260
curl http://node1:31260
curl http://node2:31260
curl http://node3:31260
```

Exposing a Service of Type LoadBalancer

If your Kubernetes is running, for example, on Azure Kubernetes Service, you need to expose the service using the LoadBalancer type, which will provide you an external IP address to be used to access the service. This will only work in cloud scenarios or in on-premises scenarios that have a Kubernetes-integrated load balancer.

Let's start by exposing the deployment as shown in Listing 5-36.

Listing 5-36. Expose nginx deployment as a LoadBalancer service

```
kubectl expose deployment nginx --port=80 --target-port=80
--type=LoadBalancer
```

Then, we can get the full service details or just the service IP address again as shown in Listing 5-37.

Listing 5-37. Get service details

```
kubectl get service nginx
kubectl get service nginx -o jsonpath='{.status.loadBalancer.ingress[0].ip }'
```

Using this service IP address, we can then access our deployment from external clients.

Summary

In this chapter, we introduced different ways to interact with a Kubernetes cluster using kubectl to get all different types of information out of it. We also looked at how to deploy and access applications using both imperative and declarative deployment methods. Let's move on to the next chapter to learn more about storage in a Kubernetes cluster!

CHAPTER 6

Storing Persistent Data in Kubernetes

In this chapter, we will dive into the need for data persistency in container-based applications and the internals of how containers persist data. We will introduce core storage concepts in Kubernetes, such as how Kubernetes stores data using Volumes, Persistent Volumes, and Persistent Volume Claims, how to provision storage, and how Kubernetes controls access to that storage. We look at both static and dynamic provisioning scenarios, specifically using NFS in our lab and Azure Kubernetes Service.

The Need for Data Persistency in Container-Based Applications

As you learned in Chapter 2, container images are read-only. When data is created or changed inside a container, the data is written into the writeable layer. The container runtime brings together both the container image and the writeable layer into a single file system seen by the applications running inside the container. When a container is deleted, both the container and its writable layer are removed, and the data inside that writeable layer is gone for good. Not the best place for persistent data, like database data. As highlighted in Figure 6-1, the writeable layer has the lifecycle of the container.

© Anthony E. Nocentino, Ben Weissman 2021
A. E. Nocentino and B. Weissman, *SQL Server on Kubernetes*, https://doi.org/10.1007/978-1-4842-7192-6_6

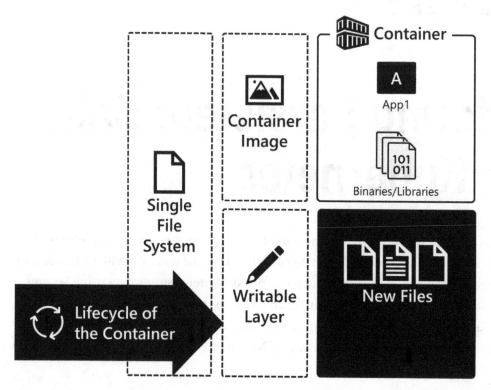

Figure 6-1. *Containers write data into the writable layer, which has the same lifecycle as the container. When the container is removed, the data in the writeable layer is also removed*

So the question is, how can you store persistent data in a container independent of the container's lifecycle? That's where Volumes come in. Volumes allow you to attach storage to a container, and any data created or changed is written into this Volume. The Volume has a lifecycle independent of the container, and Volumes are the persistent storage model used by container runtimes. Figure 6-2 highlights how a Volume is mounted into a file system giving the container persistent storage independent of the container's lifecycle.

This chapter extends that model into Kubernetes, and you will learn how Kubernetes provides storage to stateful applications running inside of Pods, which is independent of the Pod lifecycle.

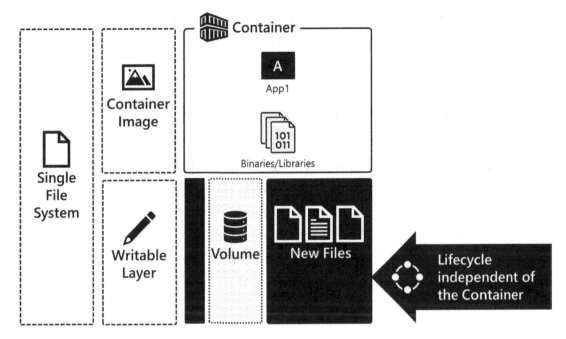

Figure 6-2. *Volumes allow containers to persist data independent of the lifecycle of the container. When the container is removed, the data in the Volume remains and can be attached to new and other containers*

Storage in Kubernetes

To deploy a stateful application in Kubernetes, there are a few core functions that the Kubernetes cluster must implement. First, the Cluster needs to provision and attach storage to a Pod as a Volume for an application. Next, depending on the application architecture, the Cluster needs to control access to that storage for both security and application compatibility. The Kubernetes API exposes several objects that enable the provisioning, configuration, and access control needed to deploy stateful applications. The following is a list of the API Objects used by Kubernetes to support stateful applications:

- **Volumes:** Part of the Pod Spec, the Volume is a storage that can be mounted by containers running in a Pod.

- **Persistent Volume:** Storage in the Cluster defined and configured by an administrator or dynamically provisioned by a Storage Class.

- **Persistent Volume Claim:** A request for storage by a user in a manifest.

- **Storage Class:** A way for cluster administrators to define classes (or groups) of storage available for provisioning in the Cluster. Storage Classes can facilitate dynamic provisioning, which creates Persistent Volume on demand to satisfy user requests for storage made via Persistent Volume Claims.

Let's now look more closely at each of these API Objects and how they enable you to deploy stateful applications in Kubernetes.

Volumes

A Volume is a storage resource exposed by the Node, mounted inside the Pod. It is a directory or block device on the Node that is accessible inside the container(s) running in the Pod. A Volume can be mounted by more than one container in a Pod, enabling sharing data between containers in a Pod. Defined as part of the Pod in the Spec, the Volume has a lifecycle independent of the container but dependent on the Pod, which means when a Pod is deleted, the access to the Volume is removed as well. However, the data on the Volume is not destroyed and is available to be attached to new Pods.

There are many types of Volumes available in Kubernetes. Each type of Volume will require unique configuration based on the kind of storage being allocated. In the following, you will find a collection of commonly used Volume types in Kubernetes. When working with Volumes, each Volume type has unique configuration attributes:

- **hostPath:** A mounted directory on the Node's file system in the Pod.

- **Local:** A mounted storage device on a Node.

- **NFS:** Mount an existing NFS export into a Pod.

- **Fiber Channel and iSCSI:** Block access to remote storage available via a storage network.

- **Cloud storage:** Access to remote storage block devices and file services for each of the major cloud providers:

  - AWS Elastic Block Store

  - Azure Disk

  - Azure Files

  - GCE Persistent Disk

- **Secrets and ConfigMaps:** Expose cluster API Objects containing configuration data into Pods.

- **Persistent Volume Claim:** A request for access to storage in the Cluster.

For a complete list, please see *https://kubernetes.io/docs/concepts/storage/volumes/*.

For Volume types like NFS, Fiber Channel, and even cloud storage, they require infrastructure-specific configuration elements. For example, when working with NFS, you will need to define the network location of the NFS server and the export you want to access. And when working with cloud storage, you will need to define a unique identifier such as a resource ID or volume ID for the virtual disk you want to access. Having infrastructure-specific configuration in Pod Specs means it can be challenging to move that code between Kubernetes Clusters since you will need to change the Pod Spec to match the storage environment of the target Kubernetes cluster. This increases the risk of errors and reduces the portability of the code. Persistent Volume Claims help solve this challenge. We will learn more about Persistent Volume Claims later in this chapter.

First, let's look at how to configure a Volume in a Pod. In the following example, we have defined a Pod running *nginx*. That Pod also has a Volume defined. That Volume is an NFS Volume with access to the file system on the storage server in our lab environment. In this example, the NFS client needs additional configuration parameters, which are the network location of the NFS server and the path that is the export on the NFS server we want to mount. It is important to call out that the Volumes are defined at the Pod level and are available to be mounted into any containers running in the Pod. In a Pod, you use the *volumeMounts* field to attach a Volume into the container. In Listing 6-1, you can see the Volume name webcontent mounted into the file system using the *mountPath* field at the location `/usr/share/nginx/html/web-app`.

Listing 6-1. Using a Volume in a Pod Spec (volume.yaml)

```
apiVersion: v1
kind: Pod
metadata:
  name: nginx-pod
spec:
  containers:
  - name: nginx
    image: nginx
    ports:
    - containerPort: 80
    volumeMounts:
    - name: webcontent
      mountPath: "/usr/share/nginx/html/web-app"
  volumes:
  - name: webcontent
    nfs:
      server: 172.16.94.5
      path: "/srv/exports/volumes/webcontent"
```

On the Control Node, let's get a Pod listing with the -o wide output modifier to get the IP address of the Pod and use that Pod IP with curl to access nginx. In Figure 6-3, we are using kubectl get pods -o wide, and in the output, you can see the nginx Pod running.

NAME	READY	STATUS	RESTARTS	AGE	IP	NODE	NOMINATED NODE	READINESS GATES
nginx-pod	1/1	Running	0	21s	10.244.1.2	node1	<none>	<none>

Figure 6-3. *Accessing nginx with the content stored on persistent storage*

In Figure 6-4, you can see the persistent storage mapping inside the Pod at /user/share/nginx/html/web-app.

```
labuser@control:~$ kubectl exec -it nginx-pod -- /bin/bash
root@nginx-pod:/# ls /usr/share/nginx/html/web-app/
index.html
```

Figure 6-4. *Viewing content stored on persistent storage inside the Pod*

In Figure 6-5, you can see where the content is physically stored on the network. It is stored on the NFS server at `/srv/exports/volumes/webcontent`. When this Pod is scheduled onto a Node in the Cluster, it is the responsibility of the kubelet to attach the storage to the Node and expose it to the Pod.

```
labuser@storage:~$ ls /srv/exports/volumes/webcontent/
index.html
```

Figure 6-5. *Viewing content stored on the NFS server*

Volumes provide a solution for persistent storage in Kubernetes. However, as you saw in the code example, there is infrastructure-specific code in the manifest. This means if you want to use this code in another cluster, the manifest needs to be updated, which increases the maintenance and decreases the portability of the code. The Kubernetes designers and maintainers saw this issue and introduced a solution to that problem. Back in the API Objects used by Kubernetes to support stateful applications, there is a Volume type listed, Persistent Volume Claim. This Volume type enables us to decouple the infrastructure-specific code into separate API Objects, the Persistent Volume and Persistent Volume Claim. Let's move forward and explore those objects in more detail.

Persistent Volumes and Persistent Volume Claims

You just learned how Volumes are used to expose storage to a Pod in Kubernetes. But you also saw that having infrastructure-specific code inside a Pod Spec increases maintenance and decreases the portability of your manifests. Let's look at how Persistent Volumes and Persistent Volume Claims can help solve these challenges and move that infrastructure-specific code out of the Pod Spec.

Persistent Volumes

A Persistent Volume is an API resource in Kubernetes defined by a cluster administrator or provisioned dynamically by the Cluster using a Storage Class. A Persistent Volume has a lifecycle independent of the Container and the Pod. Just like a Volume, each Persistent Volume has a type that defines the type of storage you want to attach to Pods. Now, rather than have the technical implementation details of your storage in the Pod Spec, when you use a Persistent Volume, the Persistent Volume object holds the implementation details of the storage attached to the Pod. Inside the Pod Spec, there is a reference to a Storage API Object called a Persistent Volume Claim. A Persistent Volume Claim is a request for the Cluster to map a Persistent Volume to a Pod.

Persistent Volumes, depending on their type, either block or file system, are mounted or attached to the Node by the kubelet. It is the responsibility of the container runtime to expose the mounted or attached Persistent Volume to the containers inside the Pod. A Persistent Volume is a non-namespaced resource in the Cluster, which means that it can be shared across namespaces if needed.

Access Modes

Access Modes for Persistent Volumes define the access pattern to the Persistent Volume object. Each Persistent Volume has an Access Mode that describes the capabilities of the underlying storage.

The following list details the Access Modes supported in Kubernetes Persistent Volumes and Persistent Volume Claims:

- **ReadWriteOnce (RWO):** Only one Node can access a Persistent Volume with read/write access.

- **ReadWriteMany (RWX):** More than one Node can access a Persistent Volume with read/write access.

- **ReadOnlyMany (ROX):** More than one Node can access a Persistent Volume with read-only access.

The Access Mode chosen depends on the application that will use the Persistent Volume and the underlying Persistent Volume storage type. For example, an NFS export can support many read/write clients due to the nature of NFS. However, like a virtual disk, a block device usually only supports read-write access for one host since the underlying virtual disk often cannot be attached to multiple hosts due to the nature of virtual disks. On the application side, applications like SQL Server can have only one process open a database file simultaneously, requiring ReadWriteOnce. On the other hand, static files such as web content can be ReadOnlyMany, and then the Persistent Volume can be attached to many Pods for scale-out access to the content stored in the Persistent Volume.

Access Modes are Node level rather than Pod level. So even if a Persistent Volume is ReadWriteOnce, Pods running on the Node can potentially access the Persistent Volume. It is up to the application being deployed and its configuration to ensure that only one Pod is accessing the Persistent Volume at a point in time.

Types of Persistent Volumes

Kubernetes supports a vast array of storage types for Persistent Volumes. In the following list are the more common Persistent Volume types we see in the field when working with stateful applications in Kubernetes:

- **hostPath:** A mounted a directory on the Node's file system into the Pod.

- **Local:** A mounted storage device on a Node.

- **NFS:** Mount an existing NFS export into a Pod.

- **Fiber Channel and iSCSI:** Block access to remote storage available via a storage network.

- **Cloud storage:** Access to remote storage block devices and file services for each of the major cloud providers:

  - awsElasticBlockStore

  - azureDisk

  - azureFiles

  - gcePersistentDisk

For a complete list of Persistent Volume types and configuration examples, check out *https://kubernetes.io/docs/concepts/storage/persistent-volumes/*.

Defining a Persistent Volume

Let's look at the code needed to describe a Persistent Volume (Listing 6-2). In the example, you can see we have defined size as 10GB in the field `spec.capacity.storage` and have defined an Access Mode in `spec.accessModes` and have chosen `ReadWriteMany`. So more than one Node in the Cluster can access this Persistent Volume. This Persistent Volume is of type `nfs`, so you see the implementation details for access to the NFS server and path. Each type of Persistent Volume has unique configuration parameters. Check the previous link for the configuration details for other types of Persistent Volumes.

Listing 6-2.   Example Persistent Volume (pv.yaml)

```
apiVersion: v1
kind: PersistentVolume
metadata:
  name: pv-nfs-data-static
spec:
  capacity:
    storage: 10Gi
  accessModes:
    - ReadWriteMany
  nfs:
    server: 172.16.94.5
    path: "/srv/exports/volumes/webcontent"
```

Persistent Volume Claims

When an application wants to attach to a Persistent Volume in the Cluster, a Persistent Volume Claim must be created. A Persistent Volume Claim is a request for storage by a user. Persistent Volume Claims enable you to just ask for storage from the Cluster rather than having the implementation details in your Pod Spec. This allows portability of your application configurations and makes your deployment manifests Cluster independent when defining Pods and higher-level constructs, separating the infrastructure-specific code into dedicated storage objects from the deployment code.

Persistent Volume Claim requests are based on size and Access Mode, and it is up to a controller in the Cluster to map the Persistent Volume Claim to a Persistent Volume. This process is called binding. A Persistent Volume Claim is a namespaced resource and binds to Persistent Volumes, which are not namespaced.

Note   When binding Persistent Volume Claims to Persistent Volumes, if the Cluster cannot find an exact match based on size, it is possible to bind the Claim to a Persistent Volume that is larger than the Persistent Volume Claim's requested size.

Defining a Persistent Volume Claim

In Listing 6-3 is the code for a Persistent Volume Claim. In the Claim, we define a size in the field `spec.resources.requests.storage` of 10GB and an Access Mode in the field `spec.accessModes.ReadWriteMany`. Once this YAML manifest is sent to the API Server, the Cluster will try to find a Persistent Volume matching the Persistent Volume Claim's size and Access Mode. This process is called *binding*, and the status of the object changes to *Bound*. The process of creating a Persistent Volume resource and a Persistent Volume Claim is called *static provisioning*. Suppose a Persistent Volume cannot be found for a Persistent Volume Claim; the status is *Unbound*. If a Persistent Volume cannot be found, this will block the startup of a Pod requesting storage from the Cluster, and the Pod will be in the *Pending* state. If a Persistent Volume is created and has no Persistent Volume Claim, its status is *Available*.

Listing 6-3. Example Persistent Volume Claim (pvc.yaml)

```
apiVersion: v1
kind: PersistentVolumeClaim
metadata:
  name: pvc-nfs-data-static
spec:
  accessModes:
    - ReadWriteMany
  resources:
    requests:
      storage: 10Gi
```

Static Provisioning for Persistent Volumes and Persistent Volume Claims

With all that theory behind us, let's statically provision a Persistent Volume and Persistent Volume Claim and deploy an application that uses those resources for persistent storage.

Static Provisioning Storage for Use by an Application

First, create the Persistent Volume using the code from Listing 6-2 (pv.yaml), and then execute kubectl get pv (pv is the alias/acronym for Persistent Volume) to get the status of the Persistent Volume. In Figure 6-6, you see the Name, which is pv-nfs-data-static, its Capacity 10GB, its Access Mode ReadWriteMany, its Reclaim Policy Retain, and its Status Available since there is no claim on it yet. Finally, Storage Class is blank since this Persistent Volume is not part of a Storage Class.

NAME	CAPACITY	ACCESS MODES	RECLAIM POLICY	STATUS	CLAIM	STORAGECLASS	REASON	AGE
pv-nfs-data-static	10Gi	RWX	Retain	Available				2s

Figure 6-6. *Output of kubectl get pv*

Next, create the Persistent Volume Claim using the code from Listing 6-3 (pvc.yaml), and then execute kubectl get pvc (pvc is the alias/acronym for Persistent Volume Claim) to get the status of the Persistent Volume Claim. In Figure 6-7, you can see the name of the Persistent Volume Claim, its status is Bound, and the Volume is the Persistent Volume it is bound to, pv-nfs-data-static. This is the Persistent Volume that was just statically provisioned earlier, pv-nfs-data-static. The Claim's capacity is 10GB, and the Access Mode is ReadWriteMany(RWX), and it is not a member of a Storage Class.

NAME	STATUS	VOLUME	CAPACITY	ACCESS MODES	STORAGECLASS	AGE
pvc-nfs-data-static	Bound	pv-nfs-data-static	10Gi	RWX		63s

Figure 6-7. *Output of kubectl get pvc. The Persistent Volume Claim is bound to pv-nfs-data-static*

When we created the Persistent Volume Claim pvc-nfs-data-static, a controller in the Cluster began looking for a Persistent Volume to satisfy the Claim based on size and Access Mode. The Cluster found pv-nfs-data-static, and then the two were bound together. In Figure 6-8, we execute `kubectl get pv` again. The status of Persistent Volume `pv-nfs-data-static` is now Bound, and the Claim is `default/pvc-nfs-data-static`. Default is the name of the namespace that the Persistent Volume Claim is in.

NAME	CAPACITY	ACCESS MODES	RECLAIM POLICY	STATUS	CLAIM	STORAGECLASS	REASON	AGE
pv-nfs-data-static	10Gi	RWX	Retain	Bound	default/pvc-nfs-data-static			64s

Figure 6-8. *Output of kubectl get pv with a bound Persistent Volume and Persistent Volume Claim*

Deploying an Application Using Persistent Storage

With the storage resources created via static provisioning, it is time to use that storage in an application. In Listing 6-4 is a deployment manifest for an application that uses storage. In the Pod Template Spec, the Volume `webcontent` is of type `persistentVolumeClaim`. The claimName is `pvc-nfs-data-static`. This is the Persistent Volume Claim object just created earlier. So this Pod will try to access that Persistent Volume Claim. Volumes are a Pod-level resource and can be shared among any containers running in a Pod. The Volume is mapped to the container through the *containers* field. The field volumeMounts specifies where inside the container's file system the Volume is mounted – in this example `/usr/share/nginx/html/web-app`. So the applications inside the container access that path, but the data is physically stored on the Persistent Volume, which is on the NFS server in the lab and at the path `/srv/exports/volumes/webcontent`. This is the default content directory for nginx. So, when the application is available, content in this directory is available via HTTP.

Listing 6-4. A Deployment using persistent storage (deployment-static.yaml)

```
apiVersion: apps/v1
kind: Deployment
metadata:
  name: nginx-nfs-deployment
spec:
  replicas: 1
  selector:
    matchLabels:
      app: nginx
```

```
  template:
    metadata:
      labels:
        app: nginx
    spec:
      volumes:
      - name: webcontent
        persistentVolumeClaim:
          claimName: pvc-nfs-data-static
      containers:
      - name: nginx
        image: nginx
        ports:
        - containerPort: 80
        volumeMounts:
        - name: webcontent
          mountPath: "/usr/share/nginx/html/web-app"
---
apiVersion: v1
kind: Service
metadata:
  name: nginx-nfs-service
spec:
  selector:
    app: nginx
  ports:
  - port: 80
    protocol: TCP
    targetPort: 80
```

In Figure 6-9, you can see our web application accessing content on the NFS server *index.html.*

```
labuser@control:~$ kubectl get svc nginx-nfs-service
NAME                 TYPE        CLUSTER-IP       EXTERNAL-IP    PORT(S)    AGE
nginx-nfs-service    ClusterIP   10.111.145.57    <none>         80/TCP     85s
labuser@control:~$ curl http://10.111.145.57/web-app/index.html
Hello World!!!
```

Figure 6-9. *Get the IP address of the Service and access the application with curl. The document returned is from the NFS server*

In Figure 6-10, you can see we have opened a bash shell into one of the Pods in the Deployment and listed the directory contents of /usr/share/nginx/html/web-app/, and the content from the NFS server is available in that directory.

```
labuser@control:~$ kubectl get pods
NAME                                   READY   STATUS    RESTARTS   AGE
nginx-nfs-deployment-557574dc8-dxwn6   1/1     Running   0          113s
nginx-pod                              1/1     Running   0          8m57s
```

Figure 6-10. *A directory listing of the mounted Volume inside the Pod*

And finally, in Figure 6-11, you can see on the storage server that in the NFS exports directory, this is the export exposed to the Pod via the Persistent Volume and mounted into the container for access by nginx.

```
labuser@storage:~$ ls /srv/exports/volumes/webcontent/
index.html
```

Figure 6-11. *A directory list of the content stored on the NFS server*

In this section, we used static provisioning to create storage for a web application deployment – creating the Persistent Volume and Persistent Volume Claim and then using that Persistent Volume Claim as the Volume attached inside the Pod.

Storage Classes and Dynamic Provisioning

Static provisioning is where the cluster administrator defines and creates each Persistent Volume manually, as we just explored in the previous section. Dynamic provisioning creates the Persistent Volume resources on demand when a Persistent Volume Claim resource is created. This can be advantageous as it relieves the cluster administrator from having to manually configure storage for user requests. To facilitate dynamic provisioning, a cluster administrator creates a Storage Class. Let's examine the details of how dynamic provisioning works in Kubernetes.

Storage Classes

To enable dynamic provisioning, a cluster administrator creates a Storage Class. A Storage Class is an API Object that describes a class of storage available for allocation in the Cluster. Storage Classes enable you to define these tiers of storage and their configuration. And then you can dynamically allocate Persistent Volumes to access that storage and attach it to Pods in your Cluster. Common ways to group storage include the performance attributes of the underlying storage infrastructure, such as Tier 1 solid-state disks or Tier 2 hard disk drives or when in the cloud Premium or Standard storage types.

The Storage Class uses a provisioner, sometimes called a Volume Plugin, which is software deployed in the Cluster that interoperates with the underlying storage infrastructure to create storage objects when Persistent Volume Claims are created and presents that storage back to the cluster as a Persistent Volume. Infrastructure-specific configuration parameters are defined in the Storage Class and used as a template for the Persistent Volumes dynamically allocated from the Storage Class. When defining Storage Classes, you can configure a default Storage Class. A default Storage Class is the Storage Class used when a Persistent Volume Claim does not specify one in its manifest.

Note   For configuration examples of Storage Classes for many different types of storage available to use in Kubernetes, check out *https://kubernetes.io/ docs/concepts/storage/storage-classes/*.

Dynamic Provisioning

With a Storage Class defined in your Cluster, when you create a Persistent Volume Claim, the Storage Class' Volume Plugin dynamically creates a Persistent Volume. Dynamic provisioning is available for many different types of physical and cloud storage such as Azure Disk, Azure Files, AWS Elastic Block Storage, Fiber Channel, GCE Persistent Disk, iSCSI, and vSphere VMDK. For a complete list of storage types that support dynamic provisioning, head over to *https://kubernetes.io/docs/concepts/storage/storage-classes/*.

Reclaim Policy

When an application is finished using a Persistent Volume and the consuming object is deleted, such as a Pod or a Deployment, the Persistent Volume Claim can be deleted. The Reclaim Policy tells the Cluster what to do with the Persistent Volume once the Persistent Volume Claim is deleted. The currently supported options are *Retain* and *Delete*. The Reclaim Policy applies to both statically and dynamically provisioned Persistent Volumes:

- **Retain:** Keeps the Persistent Volume and its underlying storage when the Persistent Volume Claim is deleted

- **Delete:** Deletes the Persistent Volume and its underlying storage when the Persistent Volume Claim is deleted

The Reclaim Policy protects reuse of the Persistent Volume object, not the underlying storage. If you use the Retain Reclaim Policy when the Persistent Volume Claim object is deleted, the Persistent Volume object will not be deleted. The status of the Persistent Volume will be *Released*. If you want to reuse the data stored in the Persistent Volume, the underlying storage needs to be manually reclaimed by a cluster administrator. You will need to delete the Persistent Volume object, leaving the underlying storage element intact. Then you will create a Persistent Volume that is newly configured to that device again. This is an entirely new Persistent Volume but just reusing the underlying storage. If you don't intend to reuse the storage, then the cluster administrator needs to delete the underlying storage.

For systems and storage types that support dynamic provisioning, the Delete Reclaim Policy is often used. The Delete Reclaim Policy deletes the Persistent Volume and its underlying storage when the Persistent Volume Claim is deleted. This requires the underlying storage to use a Volume Plugin that supports dynamic provisioning. Storage Classes often use the *Delete Reclaim Policy*, giving you the feeling of recycling/dynamic physical storage allocated to the Cluster. You will see this most commonly in cloud scenarios when using virtual disks in Azure/GKE/EKS and others. This type of functionality is becoming more common on-premises as storage subsystems begin to support dynamic provisioning. Talk to your storage administrators and vendors to see if your storage systems support dynamic provisioning.

Using Dynamic Provisioning for Persistent Volumes and Persistent Volume Claims

In this section, we introduce how to use dynamic provisioning for storage in Kubernetes in application deployments. We will present two scenarios, NFS based for on-premises lab scenarios and Azure Disk based for cloud scenarios.

Dynamically Provisioning Disks Using NFS

In the lab environment for this book, we choose to use NFS for its simplicity and accessibility... NFS is easy to configure and widely available. For production scenarios on-premises, consider using enterprise-class storage for your clusters and application data.

We just explored static provisioning for NFS in the previous section. Let's dive in on how to configure dynamic provisioning for NFS in our lab Cluster. This configuration supports upcoming demos later in the book. We also want to point out that the dynamic provisioning configuration concepts highlighted here will be like other dynamic provisioners.

We'll start with the code in Listing 6-5 to configure security for the NFS dynamic provisioner.

Listing 6-5. nfs-rbac.yaml

```
kind: ServiceAccount
apiVersion: v1
metadata:
  name: nfs-client-provisioner
---
kind: ClusterRole
apiVersion: rbac.authorization.k8s.io/v1
metadata:
  name: nfs-client-provisioner-runner
rules:
  - apiGroups: [""]
    resources: ["persistentvolumes"]
    verbs: ["get", "list", "watch", "create", "delete"]
```

```
  - apiGroups: [""]
    resources: ["persistentvolumeclaims"]
    verbs: ["get", "list", "watch", "update"]
  - apiGroups: ["storage.k8s.io"]
    resources: ["storageclasses"]
    verbs: ["get", "list", "watch"]
  - apiGroups: [""]
    resources: ["events"]
    verbs: ["create", "update", "patch"]
---
kind: ClusterRoleBinding
apiVersion: rbac.authorization.k8s.io/v1
metadata:
  name: run-nfs-client-provisioner
subjects:
  - kind: ServiceAccount
    name: nfs-client-provisioner
    namespace: default
roleRef:
  kind: ClusterRole
  name: nfs-client-provisioner-runner
  apiGroup: rbac.authorization.k8s.io
---
kind: Role
apiVersion: rbac.authorization.k8s.io/v1
metadata:
  name: leader-locking-nfs-client-provisioner
rules:
  - apiGroups: [""]
    resources: ["endpoints"]
    verbs: ["get", "list", "watch", "create", "update", "patch"]
---
kind: RoleBinding
apiVersion: rbac.authorization.k8s.io/v1
metadata:
  name: leader-locking-nfs-client-provisioner
```

```
subjects:
  - kind: ServiceAccount
    name: nfs-client-provisioner
    namespace: default
roleRef:
  kind: Role
  name: leader-locking-nfs-client-provisioner
  apiGroup: rbac.authorization.k8s.io
```

Next, we'll define the storage class itself (Listing 6-6).

Listing 6-6. nfs-storageclass.yaml

```
apiVersion: storage.k8s.io/v1
kind: StorageClass
metadata:
  name: nfs-storage
provisioner: example.com/nfs
parameters:
  archiveOnDelete: "false"
```

This specific class also requires a setting within the Kubernetes API Server. Therefore, we need to update the configuration of the API Server to support this configuration. Open the file */etc/kubernetes/manifests/kube-apiserver.yaml* on the Control Plane with privileged access and find the section in Listing 6-7.

Listing 6-7. API Server section in kube-apiserver.yaml

```
spec:
  containers:
  - command:
    - kube-apiserver
```

Within this section, add a line as shown in Listing 6-8.

Listing 6-8. New line in kube-apiserver.yaml

```
- --feature-gates=RemoveSelfLink=false
```

The changes made to this file will be automatically read by the kubelet and applied to the API Server. You may lose access to the API Server momentarily while the changes are applied, and the API Server Pod is recreated.

Note   The directory `/etc/kubernetes/manifests/` contains the static pod manifests for the cluster Control Plane. Each of the manifests in this directory defines the configuration of the Control Plane pods.

The last step for our dynamic provisioning is a client provisioner responsible for creating volumes whenever a pod dynamically asks for them (Listing 6-9).

Listing 6-9.   nfs-provisioner.yaml

```
kind: Deployment
apiVersion: apps/v1
metadata:
  name: nfs-client-provisioner
spec:
  selector:
    matchLabels:
      app: nfs-client-provisioner
  replicas: 1
  strategy:
    type: Recreate
  template:
    metadata:
      labels:
        app: nfs-client-provisioner
    spec:
      serviceAccountName: nfs-client-provisioner
      containers:
        - name: nfs-client-provisioner
          image: quay.io/external_storage/nfs-client-provisioner:latest
          volumeMounts:
            - name: nfs-client-root
              mountPath: /persistentvolumes
```

```
        env:
          - name: PROVISIONER_NAME
            value: example.com/nfs
          - name: NFS_SERVER
            value: 172.16.94.5
          - name: NFS_PATH
            value: /srv/exports/volumes
    volumes:
      - name: nfs-client-root
        nfs:
          server: 172.16.94.5
          path: /srv/exports/volumes
```

With the NFS dynamic provisioning configuration in place, let's create an application to use NFS dynamic provisioning for storing persistent data. In Listing 6-10, we have refactored the nginx deployment to use dynamic provisioning. The first part of the manifest is the definition of a Persistent Volume Claim named `pvc-nfs-data-dynamic`. In that object, you can see in the field storageClassName it references the Storage Class created in Listing 6-6, `nfs-storage`. The Volume is still of type `persistentVolumeClaim` and refers to the Persistent Volume Claim named `pvc-nfs-data-dynamic`. When this manifest is sent to the API Server, the Persistent Volume Claim is created and then the Deployment. The NFS dynamic provisioner will then create a Persistent Volume, and it is bound to the Persistent Volume Claim, and then the Pod starts up and mounts the Volume into the container. We did not have to create the Persistent Volume object directly.

Listing 6-10. A Deployment using dynamic provisioning (deployment-dynamic. yaml)

```
apiVersion: v1
kind: PersistentVolumeClaim
metadata:
  name: pvc-nfs-data-dynamic
spec:
  accessModes:
  - ReadWriteOnce
  storageClassName: nfs-storage
```

```
    resources:
      requests:
        storage: 10Gi
---
apiVersion: apps/v1
kind: Deployment
metadata:
  name: nginx-nfs-deployment-dynamic
spec:
  replicas: 1
  selector:
    matchLabels:
      app: nginx
  template:
    metadata:
      labels:
        app: nginx
    spec:
      containers:
      - name: nginx
        image: nginx
        ports:
        - containerPort: 80
        volumeMounts:
        - name: webcontent
          mountPath: "/usr/share/nginx/html/web-app"
      volumes:
      - name: webcontent
        persistentVolumeClaim:
          claimName: pvc-nfs-data-dynamic
---
apiVersion: v1
kind: Service
metadata:
  name: nginx-nfs-service-dynamic
```

```
spec:
  selector:
    app: nginx
  ports:
  - port: 80
    protocol: TCP
    targetPort: 80
```

Once the manifest is sent to the API Server, the Persistent Volume Claim is created. The NFS dynamic provisioner (Volume Plugin) creates the underlying Persistent Volume. Note that the Storage Class is nfs-storage, which is the storage class used for dynamic provisioning in this scenario.

Figure 6-12 shows the Persistent Volume Claims.

```
labuser@control:~$ kubectl get pvc
NAME                    STATUS   VOLUME                                          CAPACITY  ACCESS MODES  STORAGECLASS   AGE
pvc-nfs-data-dynamic    Bound    pvc-b22d1e5a-b9f7-4044-95e3-8490fba9b2ff        10Gi      RWO           nfs-storage    66s
pvc-nfs-data-static     Bound    pv-nfs-data-static                              10Gi      RWX                          10m
```

Figure 6-12. *The current Persistent Volume Claims in the cluster*

Figure 6-13 shows the Persistent Volumes.

```
labuser@control:~$ kubectl get pv
NAME                                      CAPACITY  ACCESS MODES  RECLAIM POLICY  STATUS  CLAIM                           STORAGECLASS   REASON  AGE
pv-nfs-data-static                        10Gi      RWX           Retain          Bound   default/pvc-nfs-data-static                            9m30s
pvc-b22d1e5a-b9f7-4044-95e3-8490fba9b2ff  10Gi      RWO           Delete          Bound   default/pvc-nfs-data-dynamic    nfs-storage            18s
```

Figure 6-13. *The current Persistent Volumes in the cluster*

Dynamically Provisioning Disks in Azure

Let's look at one more dynamic provisioning scenario, this time in Azure. The concepts here apply to any of the major cloud providers. When you need storage from your Cluster in the cloud using dynamic provisioning, the first thing you need to do is see what Storage Classes are available to you already. Most cloud providers will provide their commonly used storage subsystems as preconfigured Storage Classes for you to dynamically provision storage from.

Tip   Make sure to switch your cluster context to the Azure Kubernetes Service Cluster created in Chapter 4 (kubectl config use-context AKSCluster).

In Figure 6-14 is the output of `kubectl get storageclass` in an Azure Kubernetes Service cluster. There are five variations of storage available for dynamic provisioning, each having a different use case, performance profile, and configuration. To dynamically provision storage from one of these storage classes, you will make a Persistent Volume Claim from the Storage Class mapping to the type of storage needed.

```
NAME                 PROVISIONER                   RECLAIMPOLICY   VOLUMEBINDINGMODE        ALLOWVOLUMEEXPANSION   AGE
azurefile            kubernetes.io/azure-file      Delete          Immediate                true                  4m5s
azurefile-premium    kubernetes.io/azure-file      Delete          Immediate                true                  4m5s
default (default)    kubernetes.io/azure-disk      Delete          WaitForFirstConsumer     true                  4m5s
managed-premium      kubernetes.io/azure-disk      Delete          WaitForFirstConsumer     true                  4m5s
```

Figure 6-14. *Available Storage Classes in an Azure Kubernetes Service cluster*

In Listing 6-11, two resources are created: a Persistent Volume Claim and a Deployment. The Persistent Volume Claim defines what type of storage we want dynamically allocated for this application. So just like before, we define an Access Mode and a size. In this Persistent Volume Claim, we are also determining a storageClassName, which is managed-premium. This is the storage class that the Persistent Volume will be dynamically allocated from when this Persistent Volume Claim is created.

Listing 6-11. A deployment using a Persistent Volume Claim and dynamic provisioning of Azure storage (deployment-dynamic-azure.yaml)

```yaml
apiVersion: v1
kind: PersistentVolumeClaim
metadata:
  name: pvc-azure-data-dynamic
spec:
  accessModes:
  - ReadWriteOnce
  storageClassName: managed-premium
  resources:
    requests:
      storage: 10Gi
---
apiVersion: apps/v1
kind: Deployment
metadata:
  name: nginx-azure-deployment-dynamic
```

```
spec:
  replicas: 1
  selector:
    matchLabels:
      app: nginx
  template:
    metadata:
      labels:
        app: nginx
    spec:
      containers:
      - name: nginx
        image: nginx
        ports:
        - containerPort: 80
        volumeMounts:
        - name: webcontent
          mountPath: "/usr/share/nginx/html/web-app"
      volumes:
      - name: webcontent
        persistentVolumeClaim:
          claimName: pvc-azure-data-dynamic
---
apiVersion: v1
kind: Service
metadata:
  name: nginx-azure-service-dynamic
spec:
  selector:
    app: nginx
  ports:
  - port: 80
    protocol: TCP
    targetPort: 80
  type: LoadBalancer
```

After creating the resources in Listing 6-11, you will have a Persistent Volume, Persistent Volume Claim, Deployment, and Service for access to the application. The Persistent Volume Claim will ask the Cluster for a Persistent Volume from the Storage Class managed-premium, and the underlying Persistent Volume is dynamically provisioned.

In Figure 6-15, the Persistent Volume Claim pvc-azure-data-dynamic is bound to the Persistent Volume, which has a dynamically generated name prefixed with "pvc-".

```
NAME                                         CAPACITY  ACCESS MODES   RECLAIM POLICY   STATUS   CLAIM                                STORAGECLASS      REASON   AGE
pvc-7b2b87b3-883a-4d05-8a47-9a7496765a0f     10Gi      RWO            Delete           Bound    default/pvc-azure-data-dynamic       managed-premium            12s
labuser@node3:~$ kubectl get pvc
NAME                      STATUS   VOLUME                                     CAPACITY   ACCESS MODES   STORAGECLASS      AGE
pvc-azure-data-dynamic    Bound    pvc-7b2b87b3-883a-4d05-8a47-9a7496765a0f   10Gi       RWO            managed-premium   19s
```

Figure 6-15. *The dynamically provisioned Persistent Volume and its Persistent Volume Claim*

Note   Make sure to switch your cluster context back to your lab cluster using kubectl config use-context kubernetes-admin@kubernetes.

Summary

In this chapter, we introduced the need for data persistency in the container-based application and the internals of how containers persist data in Volumes. We then extended that model into the Kubernetes cluster and learned how to use Persistent Volumes and Persistent Volume Claims to provide storage to container-based applications deployed in Kubernetes. We also looked at dynamic provisioning scenarios in our lab environment using NFS and in the cloud using Azure Kubernetes Service.

PART III

SQL Server in Kubernetes

CHAPTER 7

Deploying SQL Server on Kubernetes

In this chapter, we will bring it all together and learn what it takes to run SQL Server on Kubernetes. We will look at how running SQL Server in a Pod is unique and how to control configuration and maintain database state. We will look at how we can leverage Deployments to upgrade SQL Server. We will finish the chapter with what considerations you need to know to run SQL Server on Kubernetes in production. We will look at things like performance considerations, resource management, and backups.

Running SQL Server in a Pod

Running SQL Server on Kubernetes is really bringing everything together that we've learned so far. We will be defining one or multiple persistent volume claims to store our SQL Server's data. We will be deploying a pod that is running SQL Server, and we will be attaching the PVCs to this pod to overcome the decoupling of data and computation in Kubernetes. As our last step, we will be exposing this pod through a service to make it accessible by other applications, as illustrated in Figure 7-1.

Figure 7-1. *Kubernetes components for a SQL Server Pod*

© Anthony E. Nocentino, Ben Weissman 2021
A. E. Nocentino and B. Weissman, *SQL Server on Kubernetes*, https://doi.org/10.1007/978-1-4842-7192-6_7

Whenever our SQL Server pod gets replaced (because it was either deleted or destroyed), it will go back to the initial state of the container image. This also means, if you did not define any persistent storage, all changes and data will be lost. The pod therefore requires three essential settings:

- **ACCEPT_EULA:** This is used for you to accept the end user license agreement, which will be set as an environment variable and is required for the Pod to start.

- **MSSQL_SA_PASSWORD:** The sa password for our SQL instance, which we will store in the cluster secret, where it's being hashed but not encrypted.

- **Storage:** The definition on which PVC to use.

Kubernetes will spin up the container, the storage is attached to the Node and then the container is started, and the mapped storage will be mounted inside the container. That way, all the data that is written by SQL Server will effectively be written to the Persistent Volume. After applying the vital settings (EULA and sa password), SQL Server will check if there are system databases in the default data directory */var/opt/ mssql/data*. If there are no system databases, SQL Server will copy a set of new system databases into this directory. If there is an existing set of system databases in the default data directory, it will bring the system databases from that directory online, followed by the user databases that have been configured for this instance.

This process will repeat every single time that our pod gets recreated, no matter if that happens because we actively triggered that, for example, by applying an upgrade, or because the Control Plane shifted the pod to another node. Using this method, you are able to decouple the persistency of the data stored in SQL Server from the lifecycle of the Pod. When a Pod is deployed, the storage is mounted, the container starts and sees it has a master database, and then SQL Server brings online the defined user databases.

Deploying SQL Server on Kubernetes

Before we can start the actual deployment, a few preparations have to be done first.

Preparation

The two essential considerations and preparing steps before a deployment can be triggered are the provision of a secret for the sa password as well as a PVC to store SQL Server's data. While there are many more things to be considered especially in a production environment, which we'll discuss later in this chapter, they form the bare minimum.

So, in a nutshell, our steps are

1. Create a secret.

2. Create storage (PV/PVC).

3. Create the SQL Server Deployment.

Storage

We will be deploying our first SQL Server to our kubeadm cluster and therefore have chosen NFS as our storage platform, which will allow us to move pods across nodes without losing access to previously generated data. As mentioned in Chapter 1, this is perfect for our lab environment but is not recommended for high-performance production systems.

For this purpose, we create a directory on our storage server called */srv/exports/ volumes/sql-instance-1*.

Save the contents of Listing 7-1 to a file named *sql-storage.yaml*. This can happen from any client, including your administrative workstation, that is connected to your cluster.

Listing 7-1. sql-storage.yaml

```
apiVersion: v1
kind: PersistentVolume
metadata:
  name: pv-nfs-sql-instance-1
  labels:
    disk: system
spec:
  capacity:
    storage: 10Gi
```

```
  accessModes:
    - ReadWriteOnce
  persistentVolumeReclaimPolicy: Retain
  nfs:
    server: storage
    path: "/srv/exports/volumes/sql-instance-1"
---
apiVersion: v1
kind: PersistentVolumeClaim
metadata:
  name: pvc-nfs-sql-instance-1
spec:
  selector:
    matchLabels:
      disk: system
  accessModes:
    - ReadWriteOnce
  resources:
    requests:
      storage: 10Gi
```

This file contains the definition for a persistent volume as well as a persistent volume claim.

Let's apply this manifest to our Kubernetes cluster using the code in Listing 7-2.

Listing 7-2. Apply sql-storage.yaml to Kubernetes cluster

```
kubectl apply -f sql-storage.yaml
```

We can verify that both have been created using kubectl (see Listing 7-3).

Listing 7-3. Verify previously created PV and PVC

```
kubectl get pv
kubectl get pvc
```

Both can be seen in the output as shown in Figure 7-2.

```
labuser@control:~$ kubectl get pv
NAME                    CAPACITY   ACCESS MODES   RECLAIM POLICY   STATUS   CLAIM                              STORAGECLASS   REASON   AGE
pv-nfs-sql-instance-1   10Gi       RWO            Retain           Bound    default/pvc-nfs-sql-instance-1                             61s
labuser@control:~$ kubectl get pvc
NAME                     STATUS   VOLUME                  CAPACITY   ACCESS MODES   STORAGECLASS   AGE
pvc-nfs-sql-instance-1   Bound    pv-nfs-sql-instance-1   10Gi       RWO                           62s
labuser@control:~$ []
```

Figure 7-2. *Output of kubectl get node -o wide*

The Persistent Volume Claim is bound to our Persistent Volume. Our storage is now ready for SQL Server.

Secret

As mentioned before, we will need to store a secret in our cluster that holds the sa password to be used by SQL Server. This secret will be stored within our cluster and can be referenced by our SQL Server deployment, so it's available and accessible for SQL Server. This also has the benefit of not having the secret in the deployment manifest, so it can be easily shared without disclosing confidential information like our password. This can be done declaratively or imperatively, but often the secret is sourced from a secure secret store, for example, Azure Key Vault.

The easiest way to create this secret is through a kubectl command like the one in Listing 7-4.

Listing 7-4. Create Kubernetes Secret using kubectl

```
kubectl create secret generic mssql --from-literal=SA_PASSWORD=SOmethingS@
Str0ng!
```

We're now ready to deploy SQL Server onto Kubernetes.

Defining in YAML a SQL Server Deployment

For our SQL Server Deployment, we're creating another manifest, which we'll call *sql-deployment.yaml*. You will find its content in Listing 7-5.

There are three specifics that we would like to point out:

- **Strategy type – Recreate:** By default, when applying an upgrade, for example, Kubernetes would run a rolling process, meaning that it would start up a new pod and try to access the database files while the old pod is still running. By setting this to Recreate, all the pods in the ReplicaSet will be shut down before creating the new ReplicaSet and pods.

  SQL Server handles this since it has an exclusive lock on the files. But it also means the container will create and restart until it can get an exclusive lock on the files.

- **securityContext:** Our fsGroup is 10001, which means that all access to the NFS will also be executed using this group. If you didn't set permissions and/or create that group in Chapter 1, this will fail.

- **Hostname:** We are not defining a hostname, so our SQL Server will be dynamically named after its pod name. We will explain later in this chapter how this could be adjusted.

Listing 7-5. sql-deployment.yaml

```
apiVersion: apps/v1
kind: Deployment
metadata:
  name: mssql-deployment
spec:
  replicas: 1
  strategy:
    type: Recreate
  selector:
    matchLabels:
        app: mssql
  template:
    metadata:
      labels:
        app: mssql
```

```yaml
    spec:
      securityContext:
        fsGroup: 10001
      containers:
      - name: mssql
        image: 'mcr.microsoft.com/mssql/server:2019-CU8-ubuntu-18.04'
        ports:
        - containerPort: 1433
        env:
        - name: ACCEPT_EULA
          value: "Y"
        - name: SA_PASSWORD
          valueFrom:
            secretKeyRef:
              name: mssql
              key: SA_PASSWORD
        volumeMounts:
        - name: mssqldb
          mountPath: /var/opt/mssql
      volumes:
      - name: mssqldb
        persistentVolumeClaim:
          claimName: pvc-nfs-sql-instance-1
---
apiVersion: v1
kind: Service
metadata:
  name: mssql-deployment
spec:
  selector:
    app: mssql
  ports:
    - protocol: TCP
      port: 31433
      targetPort: 1433
  type: NodePort
```

The most important settings, besides the ones we've already mentioned, in this manifest are the following:

- **Image:** With this file, we will be deploying a SQL Server 2019 CU8.

- **Volumes:** We're only attaching one single PVC, which matches the one we've created in the previous step. We're placing a persistent volume at */var/opt/mssql,* and anything written to that directory will be written to the persistent volume, which is the key to decoupling data persistency and pod lifecycle.

- **Service:** We're not only deploying a SQL Server pod but also a service exposing this pod. The service will be of type NodePort, so we will need to retrieve the TCP port through kubectl before, in order to access the instance.

To deploy our pod and the service, we need to apply this manifest again, as shown in Listing 7-6.

Listing 7-6. Apply sql-deployment.yaml to Kubernetes cluster

```
kubectl apply -f sql-deployment.yaml
```

After this step, we can use kubectl to retrieve the status of our deployment using the command in Listing 7-7.

Listing 7-7. Check status of deployment

```
kubectl get deployment
```

It will usually take a few minutes for the deployment to be ready, as you can see in Figure 7-3 where it shows 0/1. You may have to rerun this command a few times (or use the *--watch* switch) until it's done. Keep in mind that unless you have pre-pulled the images, the first deployment also involves downloading the SQL Server images, which will – depending on your Internet connection – take significantly longer.

```
labuser@control:~$ kubectl get deployment
NAME                    READY   UP-TO-DATE   AVAILABLE   AGE
mssql-deployment    0/1     1                 0               14s
```

Figure 7-3. *Output of kubectl get deployment*

Once this has completed, we can also check the pod's creation as well as the external TCP port through kubectl as shown in Listing 7-8.

Listing 7-8. Check status of pod and service

```
kubectl get pods
kubectl get service
```

As you can see in the output (Figure 7-4), the pod gets a unique and random name, which will change every time it gets recreated. In our example, the NodePort is 32651. We will need this for our subsequent queries to it.

```
labuser@control:~$ kubectl get pods
NAME                              READY   STATUS    RESTARTS   AGE
mssql-deployment-7c4b9d4bf-788cl  1/1     Running   0          5m1s
labuser@control:~$ kubectl get service
NAME              TYPE        CLUSTER-IP      EXTERNAL-IP   PORT(S)           AGE
kubernetes        ClusterIP   10.96.0.1       <none>        443/TCP           41m
mssql-deployment  NodePort    10.111.227.112  <none>        31433:32651/TCP   8s
labuser@control:~$ []
```

Figure 7-4. *Output of kubectl get pods/service*

With our SQL Server ready and our connection parameters retrieved, we can now use sqlcmd as shown in Listing 7-9 to run a first query against our instance.

Listing 7-9. sqlcmd query for server name and version

```
sqlcmd -S control,<PORT> -U sa -P <PASSWORD> -Q "SELECT @@SERVERNAME,
@@VERSION"
```

Note   For all the *sqlcmd* queries in this chapter, it is recommended to set up an environment variable with your password so you can use this in your queries. The same applies to the port of your instance. Also, if you prefer any other client, feel free to modify those as you see fit. Also, if you are running this command from your Control Plane, make sure sqlcmd's location is included in your PATH.

If you look at the output (Figure 7-5), you will notice that the server name matches our pod's name and the version matches what we've defined in our manifest.

Figure 7-5. *Output of "SELECT @@SERVERNAME,@@VERSION"*

Next, let's create a user database called TestDB1 using the command in Listing 7-10.

Listing 7-10. sqlcmd command to create a new user database

```
sqlcmd -S control,<PORT> -U sa -P <PASSWORD> -Q "CREATE DATABASE TestDB1"
```

If we now list the directory contents of our NFS share using the command in Listing 7-11, we will see the mdf and ldf files for this database.

Note   Run this command on the *storage* server.

Listing 7-11. List directory contents of NFS share

```
ls -al /srv/exports/volumes/sql-instance-1/*
```

You can see the output from the previous command in Figure 7-6.

```
labuser@storage:~$ ls -al /srv/exports/volumes/sql-instance-1/*
/srv/exports/volumes/sql-instance-1/data:
total 96908
drwxr-xr-x 2 mssql root        4096 Mar  1 11:27 .
drwxr-xr-x 6 mssql mssql       4096 Mar  1 11:27 ..
-rw-r----- 1 mssql root         256 Mar  1 11:27 Entropy.bin
-rw-r----- 1 mssql root     8388608 Mar  1 11:27 TestDB1.mdf
-rw-r----- 1 mssql root     8388608 Mar  1 11:27 TestDB1_log.ldf
-rw-r----- 1 mssql root     4194304 Mar  1 11:27 master.mdf
-rw-r----- 1 mssql root     2359296 Mar  1 11:27 mastlog.ldf
-rw-r----- 1 mssql root     8388608 Mar  1 11:27 model.mdf
-rw-r----- 1 mssql root    14090240 Mar  1 11:27 model_msdbdata.mdf
-rw-r----- 1 mssql root      524288 Mar  1 11:27 model_msdblog.ldf
-rw-r----- 1 mssql root      524288 Mar  1 11:27 model_replicatedmaster.ldf
-rw-r----- 1 mssql root     4194304 Mar  1 11:27 model_replicatedmaster.mdf
-rw-r----- 1 mssql root     8388608 Mar  1 11:27 modellog.ldf
-rw-r----- 1 mssql root    14090240 Mar  1 11:27 msdbdata.mdf
-rw-r----- 1 mssql root      524288 Mar  1 11:27 msdblog.ldf
-rw-r----- 1 mssql root     8388608 Mar  1 11:27 tempdb.mdf
-rw-r----- 1 mssql root     8388608 Mar  1 11:27 tempdb2.ndf
-rw-r----- 1 mssql root     8388608 Mar  1 11:27 templog.ldf

/srv/exports/volumes/sql-instance-1/log:
total 212
drwxr-xr-x 2 mssql root        4096 Mar  1 11:27 .
drwxr-xr-x 6 mssql mssql       4096 Mar  1 11:27 ..
-rw-r----- 1 mssql root       77824 Mar  1 11:27 HkEngineEventFile_0_132590716409770000.xel
-rw-r----- 1 mssql root       11489 Mar  1 11:28 errorlog
-rw-r----- 1 mssql root           0 Mar  1 11:27 errorlog.1
-rw-r----- 1 mssql root        7168 Mar  1 11:27 log.trc
-rw-r----- 1 mssql root         157 Mar  1 11:27 sqlagentstartup.log
-rw-r----- 1 mssql root      106496 Mar  1 11:27 system_health_0_132590716448350000.xel

/srv/exports/volumes/sql-instance-1/secrets:
total 12
drwxr-xr-x 2 mssql root  4096 Mar  1 11:27 .
drwxr-xr-x 6 mssql mssql 4096 Mar  1 11:27 ..
-rw------- 1 mssql root    44 Mar  1 11:27 machine-key
```

Figure 7-6. *Contents of NFS share*

We now have our first SQL Server user database online, running in our Kubernetes cluster.

Additional Configuration Options

While the aforementioned environment variables only form the bare minimum, there are a lot more, which can all be included in your YAML manifest just like the *ACCEPT_ EULA* setting. The two most important ones are probably

- **MSSQL_AGENT_ENABLED:** This is false by default. Set it to true to enable the SQL Agent service for this instance.

- **MSSQL_PID Evaluation:** This setting allows you to choose between Developer, Express, Web, Standard, and Enterprise Editions. Alternatively, you can provide a product key.

You will find the full reference of additional configuration options like collation and Language ID in the official docs at *https://docs.microsoft.com/en-us/sql/ linux/sql-server-linux-configure-environment-variables?view=sql-server- ver15&viewFallbackFrom=sql-server-2019*.

If you prefer a persistent server name over the dynamic pod name, you can specify it in your deployment manifest as shown in Listing 7-12 (the last two lines are being added to change the name of the server to *sql01*).

Listing 7-12. Define a static hostname

```
spec:
  securityContext:
    fsGroup: 10001
  hostname:
    sql01
```

To learn more about persistent server names, we recommend this blog post: *www. centinosystems.com/blog/sql/persistent-servername-when-deploying-sql- server-in-kubernetes/*.

Note   While setting the hostname manually is optional, features like replication and many third-party tools rely on this. We therefore highly recommend setting this in production environments.

Pod Lifecycle and Data Persistency

While you typically wouldn't trigger this process manually, we've elaborated on the fact before that Kubernetes separates compute and storage. While pods are ephemeral, storage is (mostly) persistent.

Let's retrieve the name of our current pod using kubectl (Listing 7-13).

Listing 7-13. Get pod name

```
kubectl get pods
```

As you can see in Figure 7-7, our current pod is *mssql-deployment-748c745b8d-w2sf8*.

```
labuser@control:~$ kubectl get pods
NAME                                    READY   STATUS    RESTARTS   AGE
mssql-deployment-748c745b8d-w2sf8       1/1     Running   0          5m14s
```

Figure 7-7. *Current Pod name*

Now, we'll use kubectl to delete this pod (Listing 7-14).

Listing 7-14. Delete pod

```
kubectl delete pod mssql-deployment-748c745b8d-w2sf8
```

Kubectl will confirm that the pod has been deleted, which will take a few seconds (see Figure 7-8).

```
labuser@control:~$ kubectl delete pod mssql-deployment-748c745b8d-w2sf8
pod "mssql-deployment-748c745b8d-w2sf8" deleted
```

Figure 7-8. *Output of kubectl delete pod*

If we retrieve our pods again, you will see (Figure 7-9) that a new pod, with a new name, has been created immediately.

```
labuser@control:~$ kubectl get pods
NAME                                    READY   STATUS    RESTARTS   AGE
mssql-deployment-748c745b8d-7pvgn       1/1     Running   0          32s
```

Figure 7-9. *Output of kubectl get pods*

Use sqlcmd to list all the databases in this instance as shown in Listing 7-15.

Listing 7-15. List databases in our instance

```
sqlcmd -S control,<PORT> -U sa -P <PASSWORD> -Q "SELECT Name FROM sys.
databases"
```

You will see (Figure 7-10) that our database TestDB1 is still present, as the storage was reattached to the new pod.

```
labuser@control:~$ sqlcmd -S control,$PORT -U sa -P $PASSWORD -Q "SELECT Name FROM sys.databases"
Name
------------------------------------------------------------------------------------------------
master
tempdb
model
msdb
TestDB1

(5 rows affected)
labuser@control:~$
```

Figure 7-10. *List of databases in SQL instance*

Upgrading SQL Server in a Deployment

Upgrading an existing SQL Server in a deployment is as easy as its initial rollout. We simply need to update the image, which you can do either by modifying your manifest's container image in the Pod Spec and reapplying or simply by setting the new image through kubectl. In our example in Listing 7-16, we will update the image of our mssql container to CU9.

Listing 7-16. Update image to CU9

```
kubectl set image deployment mssql-deployment mssql=mcr.microsoft.com/
mssql/server:2019-CU9-ubuntu-18.04
```

The key thing here is that Kubernetes will shut down the current pod before deploying the new pod (the Kubernetes default is to add one and then remove the old).

If we use kubectl to describe the deployment (Listing 7-17), we will see that the old replica set got scaled down followed by the new one being scaled up. This is again because we've set the strategy to Recreate (see earlier).

Listing 7-17. Describe deployment

```
kubectl describe deployment mssql-deployment
```

As you can see in Figure 7-11, the preceding command shows the scaling operations.

```
Type     Reason             Age    From                    Message
----     ------             ----   ----                    -------
Normal   ScalingReplicaSet  17m    deployment-controller   Scaled up replica set mssql-deployment-7c4b9d4bf to 1
Normal   ScalingReplicaSet  34s    deployment-controller   Scaled down replica set mssql-deployment-7c4b9d4bf to 0
Normal   ScalingReplicaSet  21s    deployment-controller   Scaled up replica set mssql-deployment-748c745b8d to 1
```

Figure 7-11. *Output of Listing 7-17*

This also resulted in a new pod, whose name we can retrieve through kubectl again (Figure 7-12).

```
labuser@control:~$ kubectl get pods
NAME                                   READY    STATUS     RESTARTS    AGE
mssql-deployment-748c745b8d-w2sf8      1/1      Running    0           2m7s
labuser@control:~$
```

Figure 7-12. *Output of kubectl get pods*

If you run `kubectl describe pod` on this new Pod, you can see the events that happened during and after the update command in this new Pod (Figure 7-13).

```
Events:
  Type     Reason     Age     From                Message
  ----     ------     ----    ----                -------
  Normal   Scheduled  2m20s   default-scheduler   Successfully assigned default/mssql-deployment-748c745b8d-7ng9w to node1
  Normal   Pulling    2m20s   kubelet             Pulling image "mcr.microsoft.com/mssql/server:2019-CU9-ubuntu-18.04"
  Normal   Pulled     51s     kubelet             Successfully pulled image "mcr.microsoft.com/mssql/server:2019-CU9-ubuntu-18.04" in 1m28.84489238s
  Normal   Created    44s     kubelet             Created container mssql
  Normal   Started    44s     kubelet             Started container mssql
```

Figure 7-13. *Describe pod*

Run the command in Listing 7-18.

Listing 7-18. Retrieve history for second revision of a deployment

```
kubectl rollout history deployment mssql-deployment --revision=2
```

As you can see in Figure 7-14, this will show you the details of that second revision to this deployment. Any subsequent update to this deployment could be retrieved and tracked in the same way.

```
deployment.apps/mssql-deployment with revision #2
Pod Template:
  Labels:        app=mssql
        pod-template-hash=748c745b8d
  Containers:
   mssql:
    Image:       mcr.microsoft.com/mssql/server:2019-CU9-ubuntu-18.04
    Port:        1433/TCP
    Host Port:   0/TCP
    Environment:
      ACCEPT_EULA:    Y
      SA_PASSWORD:       <set to the key 'SA_PASSWORD' in secret 'mssql'>        Optional: false
    Mounts:
      /var/opt/mssql from mssqldb (rw)
  Volumes:
   mssqldb:
    Type:        PersistentVolumeClaim (a reference to a PersistentVolumeClaim in the same namespace)
    ClaimName:   pvc-nfs-sql-instance-1
    ReadOnly:    false
```

Figure 7-14. *Output of Listing 7-18*

If we retrieve the server name and version through sqlcmd again (Figure 7-15), you will see that the server name matches the new pod name and the version has changed to CU9.

```
-----------------------------------------------------------------------------------------    ------------------------------
-----------------------------------------------------------------
mssql-deployment-7c4b9d4bf-788c1                                            Microsoft SQL Server 2019 (RTM-CU9) (KB
5000642) - 15.0.4102.2 (X64)
        Jan 25 2021 20:16:12
        Copyright (C) 2019 Microsoft Corporation
        Developer Edition (64-bit) on Linux (Ubuntu 18.04.5 LTS) <X64>
```

Figure 7-15. *Output of "SELECT @@SERVERNAME,@@VERSION"*

We can also use sqlcmd again to verify that our TestDB1 is still there (Figure 7-16).

```
labuser@control:~$ sqlcmd -S control,$PORT -U sa -P $PASSWORD -Q "SELECT Name FROM sys.databases"
Name
-----------------------------------------------------------------------------------
master
tempdb
model
msdb
TestDB1

(5 rows affected)
labuser@control:~$ ▮
```

Figure 7-16. *List of databases in SQL instance*

Note   Just as we've just upgraded our SQL Server, we could also roll back a CU upgrade using the same methodology.

Running SQL Server on Kubernetes in Production

Just like a traditional SQL Server running on Windows, there are a bunch of factors to be accounted for when designing a production environment.

Advanced Disk Topologies

Storage is always a key consideration when operating SQL Server in production. In our previous example, we've deployed logs and data to the same NFS drive including a mix of user and system databases.

Instead, you could define multiple persistent volumes and persistent volume claims and attach them to your pod, which would be the equivalent to having multiple drives on a Windows Server.

You can also use these three environment variables, to specify the default directories:

- MSSQL_DATA_DIR

- MSSQL_LOG_DIR

- MSSQL_ BACKUP _DIR

Any new user databases will be created in these locations.

Again, all PVCs will be mounted in the container at their defined locations on startup, and the master database will online the user databases.

Resource Management (Limits and Requests)

While the storage configuration takes care of our data portion, we will also need to consider compute, which effectively means CPU and memory. In Kubernetes, this is managed through *limits* and *requests,* and those can be defined on both the Pod and namespace levels.

A request is the guaranteed, minimum resource amount to be allocated. If you define a request for a pod that can't be fulfilled (e.g., requesting 128GB of memory on a 64GB RAM machine), the pod won't start.

A limit on the other hand defines the maximum that can be allocated to a resource. By default, no limit is being configured, which means that by default a pod can consume (theoretically) an indefinite amount of memory and CPU.

In the case of SQL Server, the server instance settings still apply, so make sure to set them to configure those.

The limits and requests should ideally go into your manifest (though you could theoretically set them imperatively through kubectl). They will go to a new section called *resources* for each container as shown in Listing 7-19.

Listing 7-19. Resource section in YAML manifest

```
spec:
 containers:
 - name: mssql
   resources:
     requests:
       cpu: 1
       memory: 2Gi
     limits:
       cpu: 1
       memory: 4Gi
```

This specific setting would grant SQL Server exactly one CPU core, a minimum of 2GB of RAM (which is the minimum requirement, as per *https://docs.microsoft.com/ en-us/sql/linux/sql-server-linux-setup?view=sql-server-ver15#system*), and a maximum of 4GB of RAM. The 4GB is what the container will see as its available limit. Due to the architecture of *SQLPAL*, a SQL Server on Linux by default will only see 80% of this value, which can be adjusted by using *mssql-conf*.

Note   We highly recommend to always configure a `Max Server Memory` within your SQL Server instance as well as Kubernetes limits for CPU and memory.

If you want to learn more about memory settings for running SQL Server on Kubernetes, we highly recommend this blog post: *www.centinosystems.com/blog/sql/ memory-settings-for-running-sql-server-in-kubernetes/*.

Backup (and Restore)

Of course, another important question is: How and where do I back up my data? The first part is very easy: you can use your preferred existing techniques, which can be something as simple as a maintenance plan or external tools like dbatools (*https:// dbatools.io/*) or Ola Hallengren's framework (*https://ola.hallengren.com/sql-server-backup.html*). Those backups can also be scheduled using the SQL Server Agent.

The part where it gets more interesting is the "where" part. Effectively, you are given two options:

- **Back up to URL:** Starting with SQL Server 2016, Microsoft implemented the ability to directly back up to (and restore from) Azure Blob Storage. The exact syntax and requirements can be found at *https://docs.microsoft.com/en-us/sql/relational-databases/backup-restore/sql-server-backup-to-url?view=sql-server-ver15*.

- **Attach an additional persistent volume.** Alternatively, you could attach a dedicated additional volume, which could either be cloud native (like Azure Disk or Azure Files) or any other storage system that allows you to physically store your data in a different place, like NFS, iSCSI, or Fiber Channel.

The same logic applies to restores. If you want to copy an existing backup file to your SQL instance, you can do so using kubectl. The important concept is that the file needs to be accessible to the SQL Server process.

The general syntax for such a copy task can be found in Listing 7-20.

Listing 7-20. Generic code to copy a local file to a container

```
kubectl cp LocalFile TargetPod:TargetFile -c ContainerName
```

In our specific case, to copy the local file *AdventureWorks2017.bak* to the data directory of our pod *mssql-deployment-748c745b8d-7pvgn*, the command would look like the one in Listing 7-21.

Listing 7-21. Code to copy a local file to a container

```
kubectl cp AdventureWorks2017.bak mssql-deployment-748c745b8d-7pvgn:var/
opt/mssql/data/AdventureWorks2017.bak -c mssql
```

After copying, this file can then be restored using sqlcmd, Azure Data Studio, SQL Server Management Studio, or any other client tool. We only recommend this for smaller files as you have to copy the file inside the container, which consumes space and takes time.

Note   Kubernetes is just our platform to run SQL Server – it does not replace the need for native SQL backups!

Summary

In this chapter, we've covered everything around running a standalone SQL Server instance in a pod in Kubernetes, from basic deployment over upgrades up to necessary considerations to run a SQL Server on Kubernetes in your production environment. In the next chapter, we will look at how to monitor the cluster and its applications.

CHAPTER 8

Monitoring SQL Server on Kubernetes

While we can use kubectl to look at the log files of specific pods, this simply does not qualify as a monitoring solution, and due to the distributed and ephemeral nature of workloads between nodes, pods, and containers, we really think that a central looking glass into your environment is necessary to analyze and catch issues fast enough when they occur – or even before.

Therefore, we would like to introduce you to two open source solutions that fully integrate with Kubernetes and SQL Server, Grafana for performance and metric monitoring and Kibana for log aggregation and analysis.

While Kubernetes has a built-in dashboard, it just doesn't deliver enough for a production environment.

Both Grafana and Kibana are open source tools so you can view and contribute to their code bases.

Grafana for Performance Monitoring

The Grafana Portal provides performance metrics and insights on the status and performance of a Kubernetes Node itself, as well as SQL Server–specific metrics.

Let us start by giving you an overview of the main relevant content with regard to SQL Server on Kubernetes – meaning system metrics, followed by SQL Server metrics – before guiding you on how to install and configure this solution.

System Metrics

System metrics summarize the status of a Kubernetes Node and consist of typical performance indicators like CPU, RAM, and disk usage as shown in Figure 8-1.

© Anthony E. Nocentino, Ben Weissman 2021
A. E. Nocentino and B. Weissman, *SQL Server on Kubernetes*, https://doi.org/10.1007/978-1-4842-7192-6_8

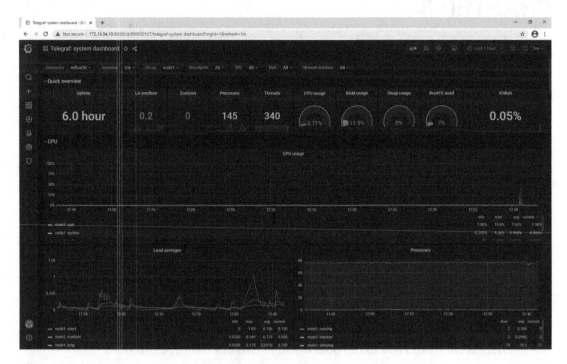

Figure 8-1. *Grafana Portal – Telegraf system dashboard*

In addition to the "big picture," you can also get detailed information for every single component like a specific disk or network interface.

When running into performance issues, this is always a good starting point. This can also be a great indicator whether you overprovisioned your cluster.

SQL Server Metrics

While the Host Node metrics are focused on the physical side of the cluster, the SQL Server metrics as shown in Figure 8-2 provide SQL Server–specific performance metrics, many of which DBAs are already familiar with.

Statistics show wait time, number of waiting tasks sorted by wait type, transactions and requests per second, and other valuable metrics. They help to understand more about the status of a specific SQL Server instance within the cluster, which can be selected on the upper left of the screen.

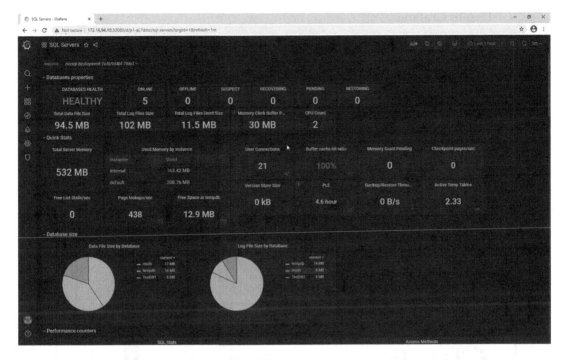

Figure 8-2. *Grafana Portal – SQL Server metrics*

How to Install and Configure Grafana

Installing and configuring Grafana is not as simple as just deploying a small pod. Grafana is the tool to visualize data, so we need two more components behind the scenes: *InfluxDB*, which is our database to store all the collected metrics, and *Telegraf*, which will be deployed to every node, collect the metrics on these nodes, and send them to *InfluxDB*.

The required steps to set up Grafana are

- Create a namespace and set is as your current context.

- Set up your variables and secrets to be used by InfluxDB and Grafana.

- Provision storage for InfluxDB.

- Deploy InfluxDB.

- Expose the InfluxDB Deployment through a Service.

- Create a ConfigMap for Telegraf.

- Create a DaemonSet for Telegraf.

- Provision storage for Grafana.

- Deploy Grafana.

- Expose the Grafana Deployment through a Service.

- Configure Grafana through the Grafana Portal.

You can see this ensemble in Figure 8-3.

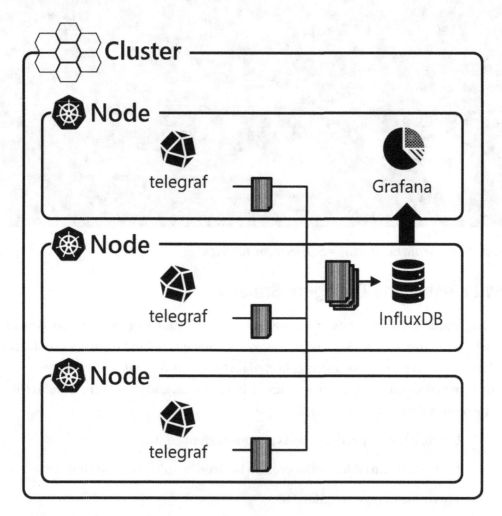

Figure 8-3. *Grafana and its required components*

We will not be guiding you through or explain every single option of rolling out these components – that alone would probably justify a book of its own – but rather guide you step by step through the required tasks to get them running in your cluster for monitoring your SQL Server workloads.

To keep things clean and tidy, let's start by creating a namespace called *monitoring* and set this as our current context using the commands in Listing 8-1. This means that every object we deploy after this will automatically be deployed to this namespace.

Listing 8-1. Create and switch to namespace "monitoring"

```
kubectl create namespace monitoring
kubectl config set-context --current --namespace=monitoring
```

InfluxDB will require a couple of secrets, which we'll set using the command in Listing 8-2.

Listing 8-2. Set variables and secrets for InfluxDB

```
kubectl create secret generic influxdb-creds \
--from-literal=INFLUXDB_DB=monitoring \
--from-literal=INFLUXDB_USER=user \
--from-literal=INFLUXDB_USER_PASSWORD=user\
--from-literal=INFLUXDB_READ_USER=readonly \
--from-literal=INFLUXDB_READ_USER_PASSWORD=readonly \
--from-literal=INFLUXDB_ADMIN_USER=admin \
--from-literal=INFLUXDB_ADMIN_USER_PASSWORD=admin \
--from-literal=INFLUXDB_HOST=influxdb \
--from-literal=INFLUXDB_HTTP_AUTH_ENABLED=false
```

The same applies to Grafana (Listing 8-3).

Listing 8-3. Set variables and secrets for Grafana

```
kubectl create secret generic grafana-creds \
--from-literal=GF_SECURITY_ADMIN_USER=admin \
--from-literal=GF_SECURITY_ADMIN_PASSWORD=admin123 \
--from-literal=GF_INSTALL_PLUGINS=grafana-piechart-panel,grafana-clock-panel
```

Up next is a set of YAML manifests. Unless noted otherwise for any of them, please save them to a file each and deploy them to your cluster using *kubectl apply -f*. These files are of course also available in the downloads of this book.

Similar to what we did for our SQL Server instance, let's create a persistent volume and a persistent volume claim for InfluxDB using the manifest in Listing 8-4. We will store that data on our NFS share again.

Listing 8-4. influxdb-storage.yaml

```yaml
apiVersion: v1
kind: PersistentVolume
metadata:
  name: pv-nfs-influxdb
  labels:
    disk: influxdb
spec:
  capacity:
    storage: 5Gi
  accessModes:
    - ReadWriteOnce
  persistentVolumeReclaimPolicy: Retain
  nfs:
    server: storage
    path: "/srv/exports/volumes/influxdb"
---
apiVersion: v1
kind: PersistentVolumeClaim
metadata:
  name: pvc-nfs-influxdb
spec:
  selector:
    matchLabels:
      disk: influxdb
  accessModes:
    - ReadWriteOnce
  resources:
    requests:
      storage: 5Gi
```

Listing 8-5 deploys the InfluxDB application and database.

Listing 8-5. influxdb-deployment.yaml

```
apiVersion: apps/v1
kind: Deployment
metadata:
  namespace: monitoring
  labels:
    app: influxdb
  name: influxdb
spec:
  replicas: 1
  selector:
    matchLabels:
      app: influxdb
  template:
    metadata:
      labels:
        app: influxdb
    spec:
      containers:
      - envFrom:
        - secretRef:
            name: influxdb-creds
        image: docker.io/influxdb:1.8
        name: influxdb
        volumeMounts:
        - mountPath: /var/lib/influxdb
          name: var-lib-influxdb
      volumes:
      - name: var-lib-influxdb
        persistentVolumeClaim:
          claimName: pvc-nfs-influxdb
```

We will expose this deployment using a NodePort service as shown in Listing 8-6.

Note   In this manifest, we're defining a static port (30010) for our service. Unlike the previously deployed services, this service will always run on this port instead of a random port. The advantage of this is that you won't have to change your URL calls.

Listing 8-6. influxdb-service.yaml

```
apiVersion: v1
kind: Service
metadata:
  labels:
    app: influxdb
  name: influxdb
  namespace: monitoring
spec:
  ports:
  - port: 8086
    protocol: TCP
    targetPort: 8086
    nodePort: 30010
  selector:
    app: influxdb
  type: NodePort
```

Listing 8-7 provides the ConfigMap for Telegraf. We've added the most common system metrics (like CPU, disk, and memory) as well as our SQL Server.

Note   Please adjust the <Port> and <Password> in this manifest to match your setting before applying it. This will be the password you've used for your SQL Server as well as its port (NodePort).

Listing 8-7. telegraf-configmap.yaml

```
apiVersion: v1
kind: ConfigMap
metadata:
  name: telegraf
  namespace: monitoring
  labels:
    k8s-app: telegraf
data:
  telegraf.conf: |+
    [global_tags]
      env = "kubeadm"
    [agent]
      hostname = "$HOSTNAME"
    [[outputs.influxdb]]
      urls = ["http://$INFLUXDB_HOST:8086/"] # required
      database = "$INFLUXDB_DB" # required
      timeout = "5s"
      username = "$INFLUXDB_USER"
      password = "$INFLUXDB_USER_PASSWORD"
    [[inputs.cpu]]
      percpu = true
      totalcpu = true
      collect_cpu_time = false
      report_active = false
    [[inputs.disk]]
      ignore_fs = ["tmpfs", "devtmpfs", "devfs"]
    [[inputs.diskio]]
    [[inputs.kernel]]
    [[inputs.mem]]
    [[inputs.processes]]
    [[inputs.swap]]
    [[inputs.system]]
    [[inputs.docker]]
      endpoint = "unix:///var/run/docker.sock"
```

```
[[inputs.sqlserver]]
  servers = [
  "Server=control;Port=<Port>;User Id=sa;Password=<Password>;app
  name=telegraf;log=1;"
  ]
  query_version = 2
```

Next, we'll deploy Telegraf through a DaemonSet using Listing 8-8.

Listing 8-8. telegraf-daemonset.yaml

```
apiVersion: apps/v1
kind: DaemonSet
metadata:
  name: telegraf
  namespace: monitoring
  labels:
    k8s-app: telegraf
spec:
  selector:
    matchLabels:
      name: telegraf
  template:
    metadata:
      labels:
        name: telegraf
    spec:
      containers:
      - name: telegraf
        image: docker.io/telegraf:latest
        env:
        - name: HOSTNAME
          valueFrom:
            fieldRef:
              fieldPath: spec.nodeName
        - name: "HOST_PROC"
          value: "/rootfs/proc"
```

```
- name: "HOST_SYS"
  value: "/rootfs/sys"
- name: INFLUXDB_USER
  valueFrom:
    secretKeyRef:
      name: influxdb-creds
      key: INFLUXDB_USER
- name: INFLUXDB_USER_PASSWORD
  valueFrom:
    secretKeyRef:
      name: influxdb-creds
      key: INFLUXDB_USER_PASSWORD
- name: INFLUXDB_HOST
  valueFrom:
    secretKeyRef:
      name: influxdb-creds
      key: INFLUXDB_HOST
- name: INFLUXDB_DB
  valueFrom:
    secretKeyRef:
      name: influxdb-creds
      key: INFLUXDB_DB
volumeMounts:
- name: sys
  mountPath: /rootfs/sys
  readOnly: true
- name: proc
  mountPath: /rootfs/proc
  readOnly: true
- name: docker-socket
  mountPath: /var/run/docker.sock
- name: utmp
  mountPath: /var/run/utmp
  readOnly: true
- name: config
  mountPath: /etc/telegraf
```

```
    terminationGracePeriodSeconds: 30
    volumes:
    - name: sys
      hostPath:
        path: /sys
    - name: docker-socket
      hostPath:
        path: /var/run/docker.sock
    - name: proc
      hostPath:
        path: /proc
    - name: utmp
      hostPath:
        path: /var/run/utmp
    - name: config
      configMap:
        name: telegraf
```

Now that we have InfluxDB storing our metrics and Telegraf collecting them for us, it's time to roll out Grafana to visualize them.

The code in Listing 8-9 will first provide us our storage for Grafana's configuration.

Listing 8-9. grafana-storage.yaml

```
apiVersion: v1
kind: PersistentVolume
metadata:
  name: pv-nfs-grafana
  labels:
    disk: grafana
spec:
  capacity:
    storage: 5Gi
  accessModes:
    - ReadWriteOnce
  persistentVolumeReclaimPolicy: Retain
```

```
nfs:
    server: storage
    path: "/srv/exports/volumes/grafana"
---
apiVersion: v1
kind: PersistentVolumeClaim
metadata:
  name: pvc-nfs-grafana
spec:
  selector:
    matchLabels:
      disk: grafana
  accessModes:
    - ReadWriteOnce
  resources:
    requests:
      storage: 5Gi
```

This is followed by deploying Grafana itself using Listing 8-10. Take note of the fact that Grafana requires its own user and group to run. We've created those in Chapter 1 when we've set up the NFS server.

Listing 8-10. grafana-deployment.yaml

```
apiVersion: apps/v1
kind: Deployment
metadata:
  namespace: monitoring
  labels:
    app: grafana
  name: grafana
spec:
  replicas: 1
  selector:
    matchLabels:
      app: grafana
```

```
template:
  metadata:
    labels:
      app: grafana
  spec:
    containers:
    - envFrom:
      - secretRef:
          name: grafana-creds
      image: docker.io/grafana/grafana:7.3.3
      name: grafana
      volumeMounts:
        - name: data-dir
          mountPath: /var/lib/grafana/
    securityContext:
      fsGroup: 472
      runAsGroup: 472
      runAsNonRoot: true
      runAsUser: 472

    volumes:
      - name: data-dir
        persistentVolumeClaim:
          claimName: pvc-nfs-grafana
```

In our last step, we'll expose Grafana as a service as well using Listing 8-11. This service will again be using a static port (30080).

Listing 8-11. grafana-service.yaml

```
apiVersion: v1
kind: Service
metadata:
  labels:
    app: grafana
  name: grafana
  namespace: monitoring
```

```
spec:
  ports:
  - port: 443
    name: https
    targetPort: 3000
    nodePort: 30080
  selector:
    app: grafana
  type: NodePort
```

Your performance monitoring environment is now ready to be used. Open a web browser and log into *http://control:30080* (this can happen on any machine that can reach the Control Plane Node and has a matching entry in its hosts file). Use the credentials that we've defined earlier (in our example admin and admin123).

Navigate to *Configuration* ➤ *Data Sources* on the left side (Figure 8-4) and click *Add data source*.

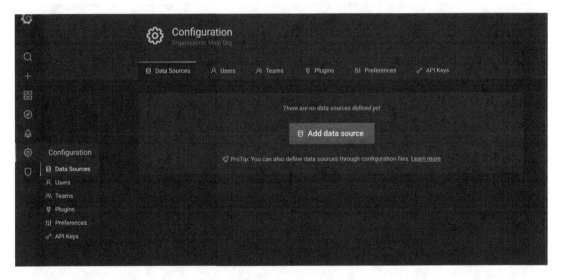

Figure 8-4. *Grafana – Add data source*

Pick *InfluxDB* from the *Time series databases* and click *Select* as illustrated in Figure 8-5.

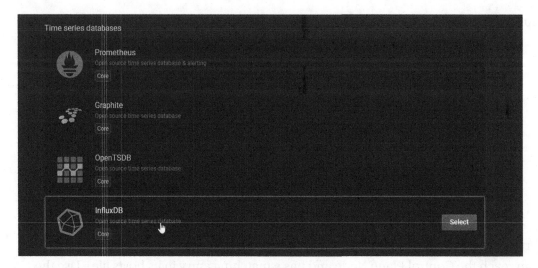

Figure 8-5. *Grafana – Add data source - Time series databases*

Set the URL (Figure 8-6) to *http://influxdb:8086*.

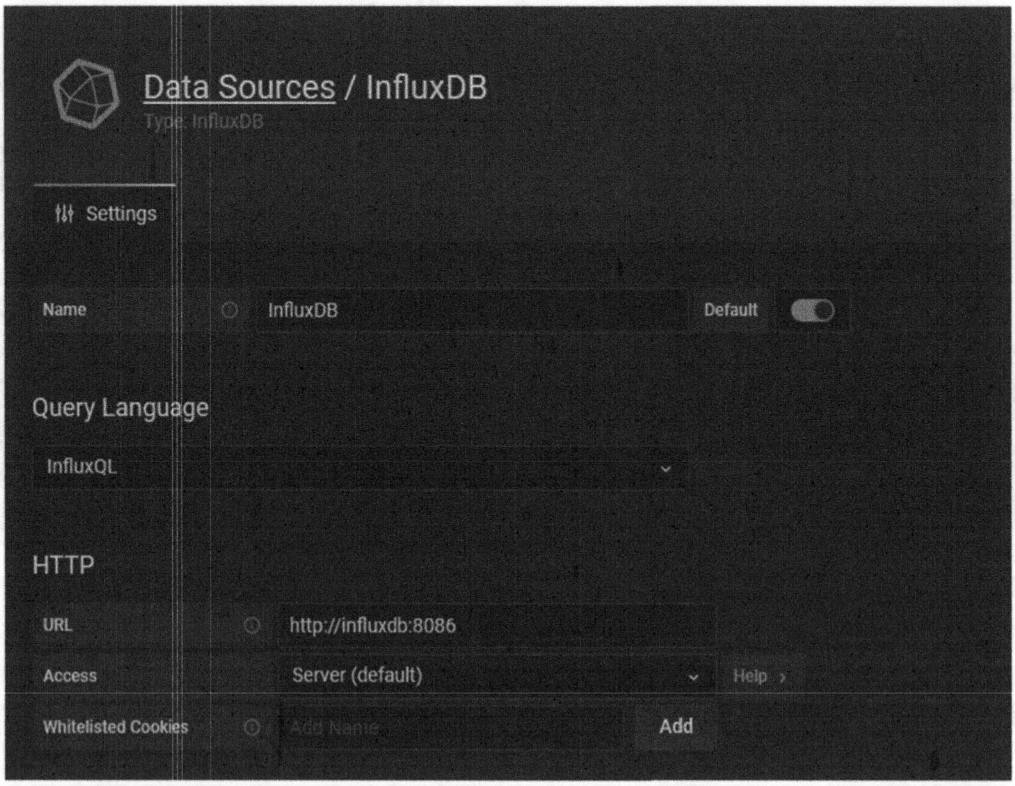

Figure 8-6. *Grafana – Add data source - Settings*

Scroll down, set the *Database* to *monitoring,* and click *Save & Test* to verify your connection as shown in Figure 8-7.

Database	monitoring
User	
Password	Password
HTTP Method	Choose
Min time interval	10s
Max series	1000

✓   **Data source is working**

Save & Test   **Delete**   Back

Figure 8-7. *Grafana – Add data source*

Using this connection, we can now create a dashboard using its metrics. Again, we won't be going through the depth of this but will rather use two existing dashboards.

Navigate to *Dashboards* and select *Manage* as shown in Figure 8-8.

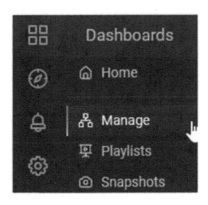

Dashboards

⌂ Home

⊹ Manage

⛶ Playlists

⌾ Snapshots

Figure 8-8. *Grafana – Manage dashboards*

On the next screen (Figure 8-9), click *Import*.

Figure 8-9. *Grafana – Import dashboard*

In the upper section, *Import via* grafana.com, enter the ID *928* and click *Load* (Figure 8-10). Dashboard 928 is a preconfigured system dashboard from the Grafana library, and we'll explain to you later in this chapter how you can find additional dashboards for you to use.

Figure 8-10. *Grafana – Import dashboard (Dashboad ID)*

Change the *InfluxDB telegraf* dropdown in the lower section of the screen (Figure 8-11) to *InfluxDB* and click *Import*.

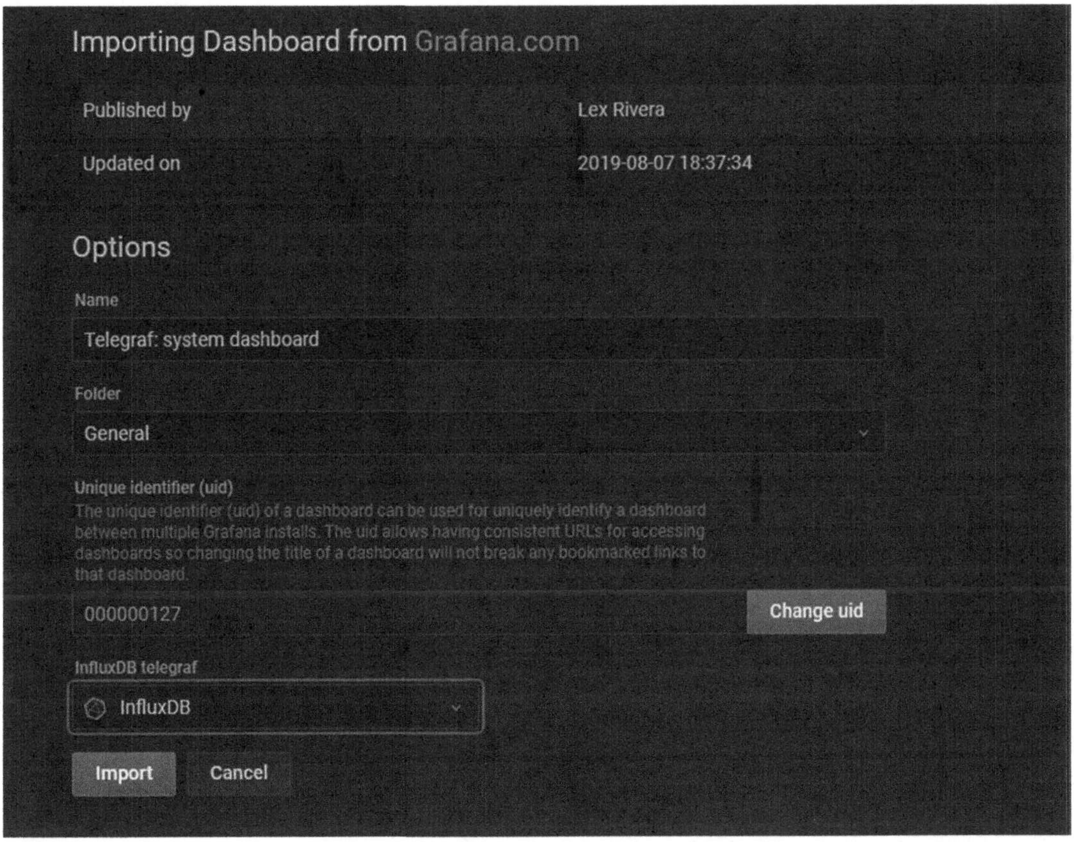

Figure 8-11. *Grafana – Import dashboard (Results)*

This will import and open the Telegraf system dashboard for you, which has a ton of valuable information about the hardware behind your Kubernetes Cluster (see Figure 8-12).

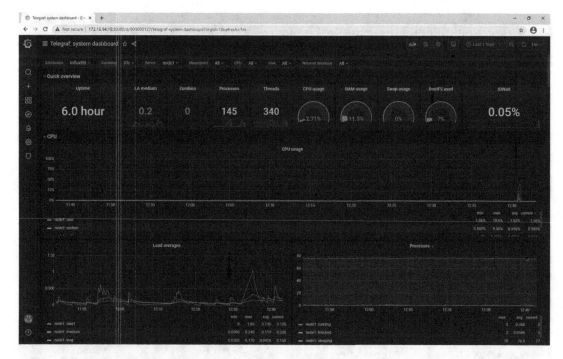

Figure 8-12. *Grafana – Telegraf dashboard*

Repeat the same steps using dashboard ID *9386* to import a dashboard that has SQL Server–specific metrics.

You will find many more dashboards that you can use at *https://grafana. com/ grafana/dashboards/*. If you want to learn more about Grafana itself, check out *https://grafana.com/*.

Kibana for Log Aggregation and Management

The Kibana dashboard as shown in Figure 8-13 on the other hand provides you an insight to your Kubernetes log files including those affecting your SQL Server pods and containers. Logging is valuable in troubleshooting scenarios, and given that logs are tied to the lifecycle of a pod and we need ways to access logs independent of that, we need a solution that covers this for us. Kibana is part of the elastic stack. It also provides options to create visualizations and dashboards on top of your log files.

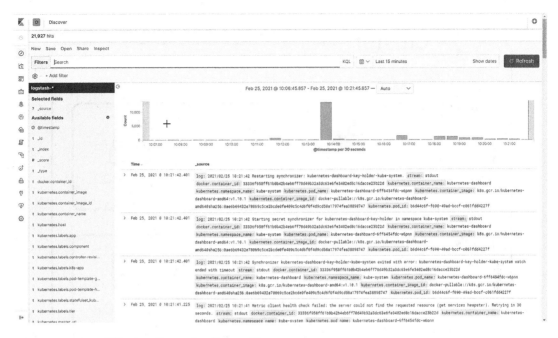

Figure 8-13. *Kibana Portal – Overview*

How to Install and Configure Kibana

Kibana uses entirely different components than Grafana, but the general logic is very similar. As you can see in Figure 8-14, we have *elasticsearch* acting as our data store, while Kibana is used as the front end. *Fluent-bit* Pods on every node are responsible to collect the logs and send them to *elasticsearch*.

The required steps to set up Kibana are

- Create a namespace and set it as your current context.

- Deploy elasticsearch and expose it as a service.

- Deploy fluent-bit.

- Deploy Kibana and expose it as a service.

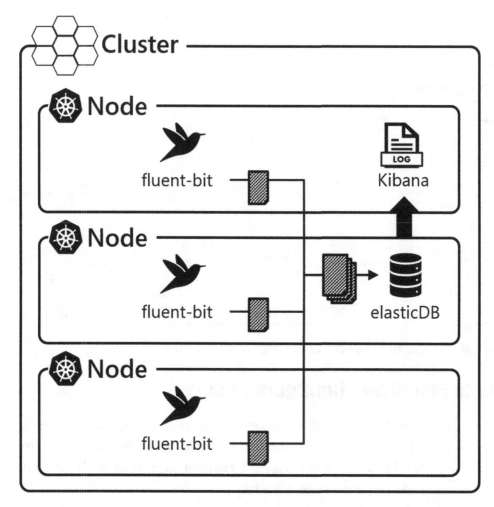

Figure 8-14. *Kibana and its required components*

Just like with Grafana before, let's create a new namespace for Kibana using the code in Listing 8-12.

Listing 8-12. Create and switch to namespace "logging"

```
kubectl create namespace logging
kubectl config set-context --current --namespace=logging
```

Also just like with Grafana, we will not explain every single detail but walk you through the steps to get your log aggregation solution deployed to your cluster.

We'll start with a service to expose elasticsearch within our cluster (Listing 8-13).

Did you notice something? We're exposing the services before deploying the pods. This is simply to illustrate that the order here does not matter. Of course, the service will only be reachable once the targeted deployment has also been created.

Listing 8-13. elasticsearch-service.yaml

```
kind: Service
apiVersion: v1
metadata:
  name: elasticsearch
  namespace: logging
  labels:
    app: elasticsearch
spec:
  selector:
    app: elasticsearch
  clusterIP: None
  ports:
    - port: 9200
      name: rest
    - port: 9300
      name: inter-node
```

Since elasticsearch uses StatefulSets, it requires one persistent volume for each pod, so instead of statically provisioning a *PV* and *PVC*, we will be using a *storage class* for dynamic provisioning, which we'll point to our NFS server again. This storage class has already been provisioned in Chapter 6.

With our storage in place, we can roll out a StatefulSet for our elasticsearch application using the manifest in Listing 8-14. In the last section of this manifest, you can see our *nfs-storage* storage class being referenced, which is how the two are being linked together.

Listing 8-14. Deploy elasticsearch as a StatefulSet (elasticsearch.yaml)

```
apiVersion: apps/v1
kind: StatefulSet
metadata:
  name: es-cluster
  namespace: logging
spec:
  serviceName: elasticsearch
  replicas: 3
  selector:
    matchLabels:
      app: elasticsearch
  template:
    metadata:
      labels:
        app: elasticsearch
    spec:
      containers:
      - name: elasticsearch
        image: docker.elastic.co/elasticsearch/elasticsearch:7.2.0
        resources:
            limits:
              cpu: 1000m
            requests:
              cpu: 100m
        ports:
        - containerPort: 9200
          name: rest
          protocol: TCP
        - containerPort: 9300
          name: inter-node
          protocol: TCP
        volumeMounts:
        - name: data
          mountPath: /usr/share/elasticsearch/data
```

```yaml
      env:
        - name: cluster.name
          value: k8s-logs
        - name: node.name
          valueFrom:
            fieldRef:
              fieldPath: metadata.name
        - name: discovery.seed_hosts
          value: "es-cluster-0.elasticsearch,es-cluster-1.
          elasticsearch,es-cluster-2.elasticsearch"
        - name: cluster.initial_master_nodes
          value: "es-cluster-0,es-cluster-1,es-cluster-2"
        - name: ES_JAVA_OPTS
          value: "-Xms512m -Xmx512m"
initContainers:
- name: fix-permissions
  image: busybox
  command: ["sh", "-c", "chown -R 1000:1000 /usr/share/elasticsearch/data"]
  securityContext:
    privileged: true
  volumeMounts:
  - name: data
    mountPath: /usr/share/elasticsearch/data
- name: increase-vm-max-map
  image: busybox
  command: ["sysctl", "-w", "vm.max_map_count=262144"]
  securityContext:
    privileged: true
- name: increase-fd-ulimit
  image: busybox
  command: ["sh", "-c", "ulimit -n 65536"]
  securityContext:
    privileged: true
```

```
volumeClaimTemplates:
- metadata:
    name: data
    labels:
      app: elasticsearch
  spec:
    accessModes: [ "ReadWriteOnce" ]
    storageClassName: nfs-storage
    resources:
      requests:
        storage: 100Gi
```

With elasticsearch running on our cluster, we can deploy Kibana and expose it as a service (again using a static port: 30445) using the manifest in Listing 8-15. This is also an example showing that it doesn't matter if we deploy everything (here service and deployment) through multiple manifests or a single manifest. Also, we're creating the service before we're creating the deployment, but Kubernetes works that out for us seamlessly.

Listing 8-15. kibana.yaml

```
apiVersion: v1
kind: Service
metadata:
  name: kibana
  namespace: logging
  labels:
    app: kibana
spec:
  ports:
  - port: 5601
    targetPort: 5601
    nodePort: 30445
  selector:
    app: kibana
  type: NodePort
```

```yaml
---
apiVersion: apps/v1
kind: Deployment
metadata:
  name: kibana
  namespace: logging
  labels:
    app: kibana
spec:
  replicas: 1
  selector:
    matchLabels:
      app: kibana
  template:
    metadata:
      labels:
        app: kibana
    spec:
      containers:
      - name: kibana
        image: docker.elastic.co/kibana/kibana:7.2.0
        resources:
          limits:
            cpu: 1000m
          requests:
            cpu: 100m
        env:
          - name: ELASTICSEARCH_URL
            value: http://elasticsearch:9200
        ports:
        - containerPort: 5601
```

Now we have elasticsearch to hold our data and Kibana to display it. The only component missing is fluent-bit to collect the logs, so we have something to work with.

In this case, we're creating everything, from ServiceAccount to Roles and the Deployment by just applying a file straight from GitHub (Listing 8-16). You could also save them first and apply the local manifests in case you wanted to check them first or make any changes.

Listing 8-16. Install fluent-bit

```
kubectl create -f https://raw.githubusercontent.com/fluent/fluent-bit-
kubernetes-logging/master/fluent-bit-service-account.yaml
kubectl create -f https://raw.githubusercontent.com/fluent/fluent-bit-
kubernetes-logging/master/fluent-bit-role.yaml
kubectl create -f https://raw.githubusercontent.com/fluent/fluent-bit-
kubernetes-logging/master/fluent-bit-role-binding.yaml
kubectl create -f https://raw.githubusercontent.com/fluent/fluent-bit-
kubernetes-logging/master/output/elasticsearch/fluent-bit-configmap.yaml
kubectl create -f https://raw.githubusercontent.com/fluent/fluent-bit-
kubernetes-logging/master/output/elasticsearch/fluent-bit-ds.yaml
```

Our log aggregation system is now ready to use. Open a web browser and navigate to *http://control:30445/*.

You'll be asked (see Figure 8-15) if you'd like to start with sample data or explore on your own, where you will click *Explore on my own*.

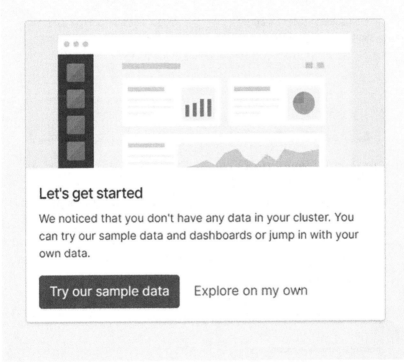

Figure 8-15. *Kibana Portal*

Similar to Grafana, we need to configure our data sources for Kibana before we can use them. As illustrated in Figure 8-16, click *Discover* on the left-hand menu.

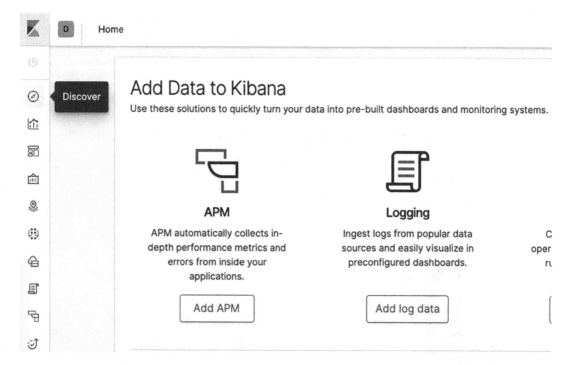

Figure 8-16. *Kibana Portal Navigation*

The configuration menu (Figure 8-17) will ask you to define an index pattern.

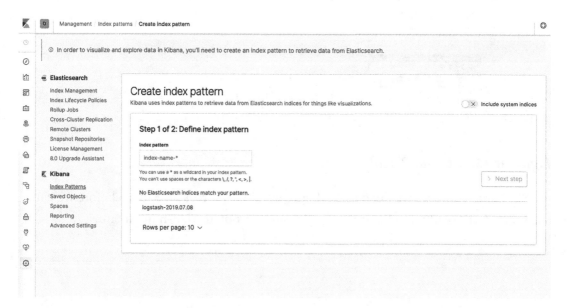

Figure 8-17. *Kibana Portal – Define index pattern*

We will keep this simple for now, so enter *logstash-** in the text box and click *Next step*.

The next step (Figure 8-18) asks you to configure which field will be used to filter log data by time. Select *@timestamp* in the dropdown and click *Create index pattern*.

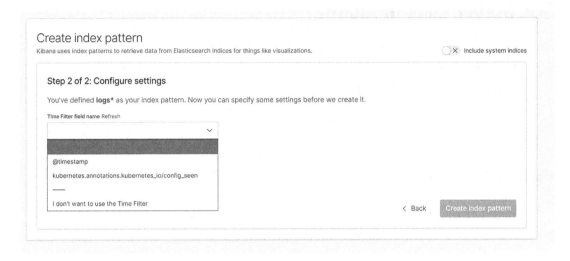

Figure 8-18. *Kibana Portal – Configure index settings*

Click *Discover* on the left side again, and you will see a histogram of collected logs within your cluster (Figure 8-19).

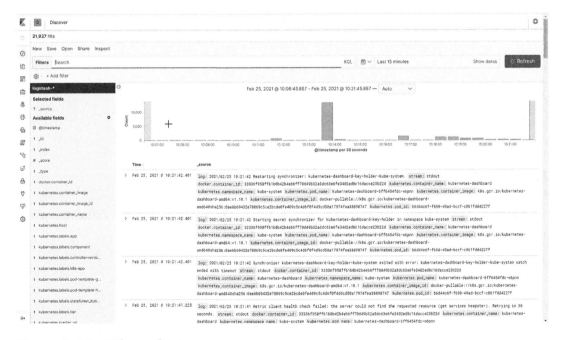

Figure 8-19. *Kibana histogram*

This data can be filtered and analyzed in many different ways. To learn more about Kibana, we recommend you to take a look at *www.elastic.co/kibana*.

SQL Server Logs in Kibana

One set of filters we want to point out explicitly though is how to retrieve the logs for our SQL Server instance in Kibana.

One very easy way would be to just use free text search as shown in Figure 8-20.

Figure 8-20. *Free text filter in Kibana*

This will involve a lot of unwanted noise though. The better solution is to add a proper filter. To do so, click *Add filter* below the filter bar as shown in Figure 8-21.

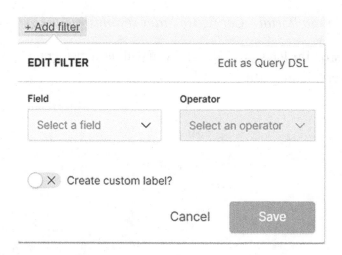

Figure 8-21. *Add filter in Kibana*

Select the Field *kuberneters.container_name*, the Operator *is,* and the Value *mssql* as shown in Figure 8-22 and click *Save.*

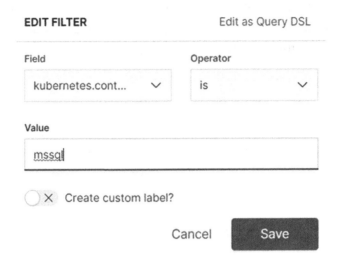

Figure 8-22. Add filter for mssql in Kibana

This will bring up log files from all our SQL Server containers, as shown in Figure 8-23.

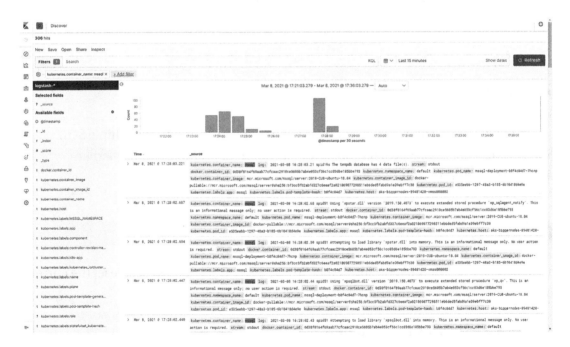

Figure 8-23. Filter for mssql in Kibana

Of course, this can also be combined with the free text filter. If you add *"Login failed"* to the filter as shown in Figure 8-24, you will get all failed login events in our SQL Server, as this log also includes the full SQL Server Error Log.

Figure 8-24. *SQL Server Error Log in Kibana*

In our example, that is already sufficient. In case you are running multiple SQL Server instances, you could also add additional filters for settings like *namespace*, *deployment,* or *pod* name.

Cleanup

To make sure that your upcoming demos run in the correct namespace, reset the current context to the default namespace as shown in Listing 8-17.

Listing 8-17. Reset kubectl context

```
kubectl config set-context --current --namespace=default
```

Note The ports used in this example will also be used by services in the upcoming chapters. Either keep that in mind and modify the ports in those chapters or delete the resources from this chapter first.

Summary

In this chapter, we've covered ways on how to monitor the cluster and its applications using Grafana and the Kibana dashboard. We then used those portals to gain insights about our previously deployed SQL Server on Kubernetes. Let's move on to the next chapter to look at Azure Arc–enabled Data Services, which allow us to deploy SQL Server on Kubernetes with high-availability options.

CHAPTER 9

Azure Arc–Enabled Data Services and High Availability for SQL Server on Kubernetes

This chapter introduces Azure Arc–enabled Data Services and the powerful capabilities they provide to deploy and manage local, on-premises, and hybrid cloud data resources using the same automation and centralized control management and tooling that you get from the Azure Cloud. We will show you how to deploy and manage databases running on SQL Server in your corporate data center as if they were part of the Azure platform, all using the power of Kubernetes. Azure Arc–enabled Data Services are also the answer to the question how to implement availability groups (AGs) for SQL Server (using Managed Instances) on Kubernetes.

What's Azure Arc?

At its core, Microsoft Azure Arc provides Azure management services wherever you have deployed resources on-premises or any cloud. It enables you to have consistent management services and tooling for your organizations' core operations across technology architectures wherever deployed. Let's look at the core features of Azure Arc:

- **Unified experience across on-premises and hybrid cloud:** Familiar tools like Azure Portal, the Azure CLI, PowerShell, and REST API are available to you to manage and deploy systems.

© Anthony E. Nocentino, Ben Weissman 2021
A. E. Nocentino and B. Weissman, *SQL Server on Kubernetes*, https://doi.org/10.1007/978-1-4842-7192-6_9

- **Deployment and operations:** With a unified set of tools, deployments and operations are consistent wherever you deploy, on-premises or in any cloud. Unified tooling enables your organization to use the same code and tools in any deployment scenario wherever deployed. A pivotal element to operations is performance and availability monitoring, and Azure Monitor is available to help you do that for your Azure Arc–enabled resources.

- **Consolidated access controls, security, policy management, and logging:** Implementing more than one security model based on where your resources are deployed is challenging and risky since you potentially have to manage multiple sets of security rules and their implementations. Azure Arc enables you to have a consolidated security model and implementation and use tools like Azure Log Analytics for centralized security and application logs. Additionally, you can manage governance and control solutions with services like Azure Policy.

- **Inventory and organization:** With one set of tooling available and key Azure constructs such as resource groups, subscriptions, and tags, administrators, operators, and managers can get a complete view of their technology estate. It doesn't matter anymore where systems are deployed – services and resources are registered as managed resources in Azure irrespective of where they are deployed, on-premises or in any cloud.

Azure Arc ranges from offerings like *Azure Arc-enabled servers* and *Azure Arc-enabled Kubernetes* to *Azure Arc-enabled SQL Server* and *Azure Arc-enabled Data Services*.

Given the scope of this book though, let's sum this up to its essence: Azure Arc is a range of services that allow you to run services that formerly were only deployable to Microsoft's Azure Cloud to any infrastructure in any cloud. We will focus on some of the offerings within Azure Arc–enabled Data Services over the course of this chapter.

To learn more about Azure Arc in general, please refer to *https://docs.microsoft.com/en-us/azure/azure-arc/*.

Introduction to Azure Arc–Enabled Data Services

Azure Arc–enabled Data Services architecture is a layered architecture of hardware, Kubernetes, Management Control Plane, and Data Services. Figure 9-1 highlights the architecture.

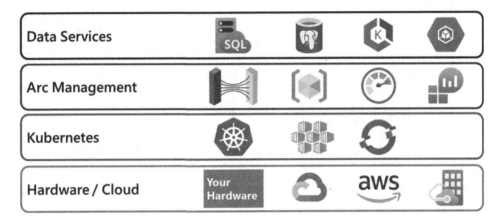

Figure 9-1. *Azure Arc–enabled Data Services architecture*

The foundational layer is Kubernetes running on any hardware, which can be either on-premises or in any cloud and built on either physical or virtual machines. Then, deployed inside the Kubernetes Cluster is the Arc Management Control Plane. The Arc Management Control Plane is Azure Arc's brains and extends Azure Resource Manager (ARM) to your on-premises or hybrid cloud deployments. And on top of all of that are Azure Arc–enabled Data Services.

Let us take a closer look at the core components of Azure Arc–enabled Data Services as illustrated in Figure 9-2.

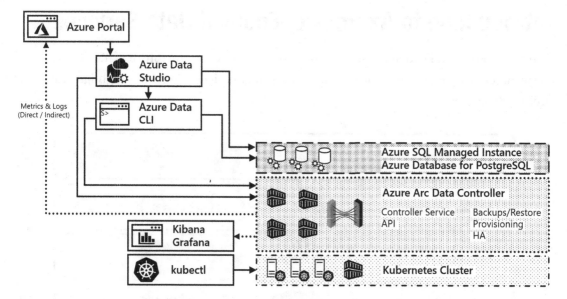

Figure 9-2. *Core components of Azure Arc–enabled Data Services*

Azure Arc Data Controller

Besides the Kubernetes cluster, the first component we need to run Azure Arc–enabled Data Services is the Data Controller. It provides the connectivity to Azure Portal and deploys some core services that we need to provision services later.

Monitoring (Grafana and Kibana)

In the last chapter, we deployed Grafana, and as you remember, there were quite a few steps involved. Good news: When you deploy an Azure Arc Data Controller, it will automatically deploy a Grafana dashboard including its prerequisites for you.

It also comes with preconfigured dashboards like the SQL Managed Instance Metrics, as shown in Figure 9-3. This looks different from the examples we've seen in the previous chapter because this dashboard is tailored to the specifics of a SQL Managed Instance.

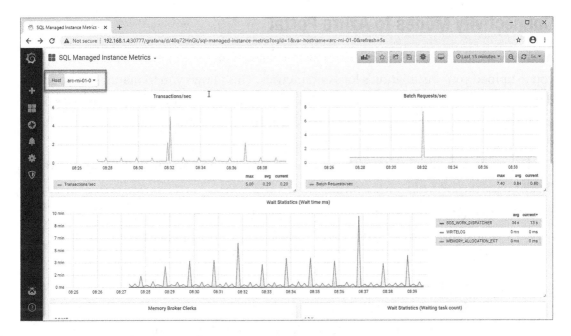

Figure 9-3. *Grafana Portal – SQL MI Metrics*

In addition to this dashboard, the dashboards shown in Figure 9-4 are automatically deployed.

Figure 9-4. *Built-in dashboards in Grafana Portal*

Of course, you can add any existing dashboard or create your own just like we did in the previous chapter as well.

In addition to Grafana, Azure Arc–enabled Data Services also come with Kibana and its prerequisites rolled out by default, so there is also no need to deploy that manually.

Connectivity Modes to Azure Portal

Azure Arc–enabled Data Services come with a backchannel to Azure Portal, allowing you to upload your installation's logs and metrics. This allows you to manage all your data estate – no matter if it's a Managed Instance running in Azure Arc on-premises or an Azure SQL DB in Azure – in one single place. This information is also used for billing purposes.

Depending on your infrastructure, location, and needs, you can pick between two modes:

- **Directly connected:** In this mode, your logs and metrics are constantly sent to Azure Portal, making the data available for analysis almost instantly.

- **Indirectly connected:** In this mode, you need to manually trigger or schedule an export and upload of your metrics and logs. This is especially useful if you are in a location with limited Internet connectivity.

Once a resource's data has been uploaded to Azure, it will show in the portal as you can see in the example in Figure 9-5.

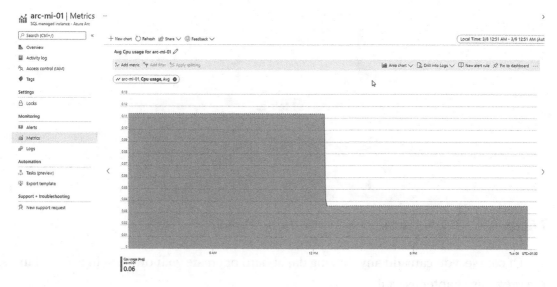

Figure 9-5. *CPU metric showing in Azure Portal*

Data Services

On top of our Data Controller sit the Data Services which at the time of writing can either be an *Azure Arc SQL Managed Instance* or *Azure Database for PostgreSQL*.

We will only be focusing on SQL Managed Instances as PostgreSQL is beyond the scope of this book.

Azure Arc SQL Managed Instance

Azure Arc-enabled SQL Managed Instance is your lift and shift version of SQL Server. It enables you to move workloads seamlessly into Azure Arc as it provides a high level of compatibility with on-premises installations of SQL Server, which is documented as nearly 100% compatible. This means that moving your databases from their current on-premises implementations into Azure Arc–enabled SQL Managed Instance will require little to no database changes. When deploying an Azure Arc–enabled SQL Managed Instance, you can take a backup from an on-premises version of SQL Server and restore that backup directly to an Azure Arc-enabled SQL Managed Instance.

Tip   Following *https://docs.microsoft.com/en-us/azure/azure-arc/ data/managed-instance-features#Unsupported*, you will find the list of unsupported features and services for Azure Arc–enabled SQL Managed Instance.

Azure Arc–enabled SQL Managed Instance runs as a SQL Server on Linux process inside a container in Kubernetes. The features not available are similar to those not supported in SQL Server on Linux. For more information, look at *https://docs. microsoft.com/en-us/sql/linux/sql-server-linux-editions-and-components-2019?#Unsupported*.

Similar to the Always Current or Evergreen SQL offerings available in Azure PaaS services such as Azure SQL Managed Instance in Azure Cloud–hosted deployments, Microsoft will continuously publish updated SQL Managed Instance container images to the Microsoft Container Registry for Azure Arc–enabled SQL Managed Instance. Then, based on update policies defined in your deployment, you can specify how often and when the updates are applied to your environment. In traditional implementations of SQL Server, managing updates is a challenging and time-consuming process. Kubernetes provides the ability to absorb updates and changes quickly and roll them out into the cluster. This is the update model used in Azure Arc–enabled Data Services.

Azure Database for PostgreSQL

The other service currently available within Azure Arc–enabled Data Services is Azure Database for PostgreSQL. We will not be going into more details on this, as it is beyond the scope of this book.

Kubernetes Constructs in Azure Arc–Enabled Data Services

Of course, we also want to know how all this is being reflected by Kubernetes constructs.

Every deployment of Azure Arc-enabled Data Services will live in its own namespace. This will allow you to run multiple deployments on the same Kubernetes cluster.

As you can see in Figure 9-6, in such a namespace, we will find the pods of the controller, Grafana, Kibana, and the other Data Controller services as well as the Data Services associated with this controller.

```
C:\Users\arc>kubectl get pods -n arc
NAME                READY   STATUS    RESTARTS   AGE
arc-mi-01-0         3/3     Running   0          5m10s
bootstrapper-nbv22  1/1     Running   0          16m
control-tls4h       2/2     Running   0          16m
controldb-0         2/2     Running   0          12m
controlwd-1125r     1/1     Running   0          11m
logsdb-0            1/1     Running   0          11m
logsui-z4nmz        1/1     Running   0          11m
metricsdb-0         1/1     Running   0          11m
metricsdc-69g5r     1/1     Running   0          11m
metricsdc-jgp28     1/1     Running   0          11m
metricsdc-vgx97     1/1     Running   0          11m
metricsui-9pqpj     1/1     Running   0          11m
mgmtproxy-74qwn     2/2     Running   0          11m
```

Figure 9-6. *Pods in Azure Arc-enabled Data Services namespace*

Access to the Data Services and monitoring and logging applications in the pods is exposed through Kubernetes Services as shown in Figure 9-7.

```
C:\Users\arc>kubectl get svc -n arc
NAME                        TYPE           CLUSTER-IP      EXTERNAL-IP      PORT(S)                                          AGE
arc-mi-01-external-svc      LoadBalancer   10.0.222.189    52.191.230.91    1433:30251/TCP                                   4m39s
arc-mi-01-svc               ClusterIP      None            <none>           1433/TCP                                         4m39s
controldb-svc               ClusterIP      10.0.36.202     <none>           1433/TCP,8311/TCP,8411/TCP                       15m
controller-svc              ClusterIP      10.0.94.113     <none>           443/TCP,8311/TCP,8301/TCP,8411/TCP,8401/TCP      15m
controller-svc-external     LoadBalancer   10.0.243.50     52.191.226.145   30080:31649/TCP                                  15m
logsdb-svc                  ClusterIP      10.0.248.89     <none>           9200/TCP,8300/TCP,8400/TCP                       10m
logsui-svc                  ClusterIP      10.0.107.69     <none>           5601/TCP,8300/TCP,8400/TCP                       10m
metricsdb-svc               ClusterIP      10.0.160.253    <none>           8086/TCP,8300/TCP,8400/TCP                       10m
metricsdc-svc               ClusterIP      10.0.200.120    <none>           8300/TCP,8400/TCP                                10m
metricsui-svc               ClusterIP      10.0.39.5       <none>           3000/TCP,8300/TCP,8400/TCP                       10m
mgmtproxy-svc               ClusterIP      10.0.30.53      <none>           443/TCP,8300/TCP,8311/TCP,8400/TCP,8411/TCP      10m
mgmtproxy-svc-external      LoadBalancer   10.0.34.218     52.191.230.75    30777:30048/TCP                                  10m
```

Figure 9-7. *Services in Azure Arc–enabled Data Services namespace*

To allow for maximum flexibility, Azure Arc-enabled Data Services require at least one storage class. Whenever a Data Controller or data service is created, a storage class is required. This class can be different between different services, and each service can use different classes for logs (Kubernetes logs), data, and data logs.

If you want to learn more about Azure Arc-enabled Data Services, we also recommend our Apress book *Azure Arc–Enabled Data Services Revealed*.

Deploying Azure Arc–Enabled Data Services

Now it's time to deploy some Azure Arc-enabled Data Services.

Prerequisites

As expected, we need a couple of prerequisites before we can start the deployment process.

Kubernetes Cluster

As you probably guessed based on the architecture, a Kubernetes cluster is required.

As mentioned before, within this cluster, we also need at least one storage class that allows dynamic provisioning (like the NFS provisioner we used when we deployed *elasticsearch* in Chapter 8).

We will be using our *AKSCluster* for this deployment. If you prefer using your *kubeadm* cluster, just adjust the *storage class* accordingly.

Therefore, we start by switching our kubectl context back to the AKSCluster as shown in Listing 9-1.

Listing 9-1. Switch kubectl context to AKSCluster

```
kubectl config use-context AKSCluster
```

We will also retrieve the storage classes in this cluster using the kubectl command in Listing 9-2.

Listing 9-2. List storage classes in AKSCluster

```
kubectl get storageclass
```

Unless you've deployed any additional storage classes to this cluster, this should look like the output in Figure 9-8.

```
C:\Users\labuser>kubectl get storageclass
NAME                PROVISIONER                RECLAIMPOLICY   VOLUMEBINDINGMODE     ALLOWVOLUMEEXPANSION   AGE
azurefile           kubernetes.io/azure-file   Delete          Immediate            true                   7m36s
azurefile-premium   kubernetes.io/azure-file   Delete          Immediate            true                   7m36s
managed             kubernetes.io/azure-disk   Delete          WaitForFirstConsumer true                   7m36s
managed-premium     kubernetes.io/azure-disk   Delete          WaitForFirstConsumer true                   7m36s
```

Figure 9-8. *Storage classes in AKS Cluster*

Tooling

While we could deploy everything in the Azure Arc ecosystem through YAML manifests, Microsoft makes our life easier by providing another level of abstraction. Using a tool called azdata, we can describe the environment and services we require, which will generate the objects in Kubernetes for us. For more complex scenarios, those can be configured through JSON files, whereas simpler use cases can be run through command line parameters, very similar to the concept of imperative vs. declarative statements with kubectl.

Note   Don't confuse the *Azure CLI* and *azdata*. They are two different tools!

We have already installed azdata on our administrative workstation in Chapter 1.

Should you prefer a graphical experience, Azure Data Studio also provides a graphical installation wizard. This wizard will create a Jupyter notebook for each deployment calling azdata in the background. In this book however, we will focus on the command line–based installation.

Deploying a Data Controller

Once you have azdata installed and your kubectl context set to the right cluster, an Azure Arc Data Controller can be deployed through a command like the one in Listing 9-3.

You will need to provide the following settings:

- **Name:** Name of the controller.

- **Namespace:** Namespace within your Kubernetes Cluster to be used – this namespace can't have any other objects. If it doesn't exist yet, it will be created.

- **Subscription:** Your Azure subscription ID.

- **Resource group:** The resource group in Azure where the service should show up after deployment.

- **Location:** The Azure region for your metrics and logs.

- **Storage class:** The storage class for the Data Controller's data and logs. If this is omitted, the default class will be used.

- **Profile name:** The deployment profile to be used .

Listing 9-3. azdata command to create a Data Controller

```
azdata arc dc create \
--connectivity-mode Indirect \
--name arc-dc-aks \
--namespace arc \
--subscription <Subscription ID> \
--resource-group "Kubernetes-Cloud" \
--location eastus \
--storage-class managed-premium \
--profile-name azure-arc-aks-premium-storage
```

If you are deploying to another target than AKS, you will need to adjust the *profile name* accordingly. A list of available profiles can be retrieved using the command in Listing 9-4.

Note   Our example is using indirect mode, and if you want to upload your metrics and logs to Azure Portal, additional steps that are out of scope of this book are required.

Listing 9-4.   azdata command to list profile names for Data Controller

```
azdata arc dc config list
```

The output will look similar to the one shown in Figure 9-9.

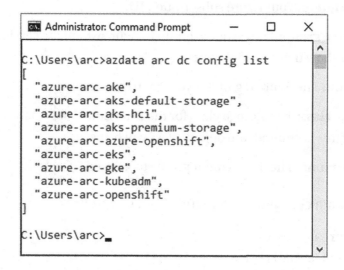

Figure 9-9.   *List of configuration profiles for Azure Arc Data Controllers*

To deploy a Data Controller, you need to accept the license agreement and provide a username and password.

If you want to avoid being prompted for them when running the azdata command, you can also provide them in three environment variables:

- **ACCEPT_EULA:** To be set to "Y" (this is only required for the deployment of data services like a SQL Managed Instance, not for the Data Controller)

- **AZDATA_USERNAME:** The username to be used, for example, arcadmin

- **AZDATA_PASSWORD:** To be a strong password of your choice

If you want to follow the creation of Pods while deploying through azdata, you can do so using the command in Listing 9-5.

Listing 9-5. Monitor deployment status using kubectl

```
kubectl get pods -n arc –watch
```

Note   Whenever you add the *--watch* switch to a *kubectl get* statement, kubectl will keep monitoring the objects matching your command and constantly refresh you on their current state.

---

azdata will report back once the deployment has completed as shown in Figure 9-10.

```
Data controller username:arcadmin
Data controller password:
Confirm Data controller password:

Deploying data controller

NOTE: Data controller creation can take a significant amount of time depending on
configuration, network speed, and the number of nodes in the cluster.

Data controller endpoint is available at https://52.224.73.27:30080
3 out of 9 resources are ready.
4 out of 9 resources are ready.
7 out of 9 resources are ready.
7 out of 9 resources are ready.
Waiting for data controller to be ready after 5 minutes.
7 out of 9 resources are ready.
9 out of 9 resources are ready.
Data controller successfully deployed.
```

Figure 9-10. *Output of a Data Controller deployment*

Deploying an Azure Arc–Enabled SQL Managed Instance

To deploy an Azure Arc–enabled SQL Managed Instance through azdata, we first need to log into our cluster, as shown in Listing 9-6.

Listing 9-6. azdata command to log into your Data Controller

```
azdata login -ns arc
```

> **Note**   If you did not store your username and password in environment variables, this command will prompt you for them again.

A new Managed Instance can be deployed through a simple azdata command like the one in Listing 9-7. The only required parameter is the name of the instance. If you do not provide storage classes, the default class will be used. This requires a default storage class to be defined!

Listing 9-7. azdata command to create a new SQL Managed Instance with parameters

```
azdata arc sql mi create \
        --name arc-mi-01 \
        --storage-class-data managed-premium \
        --storage-class-logs managed-premium \
        --storage-class-data-logs managed-premium \
        --storage-class-backups managed-premium
```

The deployment requires a username and password again, which will be prompted for unless you've provided them through environment variables.

Once the deployment has completed, azdata will report back as shown in Figure 9-11.

```
C:\Users\labuser>azdata arc sql mi create --name arc-mi-01 --storage-class-data managed-premium
--storage-class-logs managed-premium --storage-class-data-logs managed-premium
Arc SQL managed instance username:admin
Arc SQL managed instance password:
Confirm Arc SQL managed instance password:
Deploying arc-mi-01 in namespace `arc`
arc-mi-01 is Ready
```

Figure 9-11. *Output of azdata after creation of MI*

Look at the pods using the code in Listing 9-8.

Listing 9-8. kubectl get pods

```
kubectl get pods arc-mi-01-0 -n arc
```

We can also see the pod that has been created for our Managed instance (Figure 9-12).

```
C:\Users\labuser>kubectl get pods arc-mi-01-0 -n arc
NAME          READY   STATUS    RESTARTS   AGE
arc-mi-01-0   3/3     Running   0          6m15s
```

Figure 9-12. *Pod for MI*

Note   This is one single pod with three containers running inside it. This does not mean we're getting three SQL Server instances.

To connect to our instance using *sqlcmd, Azure Data Studio,* or another client tool, we need the IP address and the port of the SQL Server endpoint. Besides using kubectl to list the services, we can also use the *azdata* command in Listing 9-9 for this purpose.

Listing 9-9. azdata command to list all SQL MIs in the current controller

```
azdata arc sql mi list
```

This will return our instance's external endpoint, its name, the number of replicas, and its current state as shown in Figure 9-13.

```
ExternalEndpoint     Name        Replicas     State
------------------   ---------   ----------   --------
52.191.230.91,1433   arc-mi-01   1/1          Ready
```

Figure 9-13. *Managed Instances in Azure Arc namespace*

We could now use this information and connect to our SQL Server.

High Availability for an Azure Arc SQL Managed Instance

At the time of writing, a "regular" SQL Server on Kubernetes, like the one we've deployed in Chapter 7, does not support *availability groups.*

You may now be wondering why you even need an AG since Kubernetes is providing native high availability. The problem is depending on what kind of storage you are using, in the case of a node failure, the storage needs to be attached to a new node. This can take anywhere from milliseconds to minutes. Having a downtime of multiple minutes is obviously not acceptable in an HA environment.

The answer to that also lies in Arc through *SQL Managed Instance Always On availability groups.* As you can see in Figure 9-14, they bring together Azure Arc SQL Managed Instances, which we've introduced earlier in this chapter, and availability groups *(AGs)* for high availability.

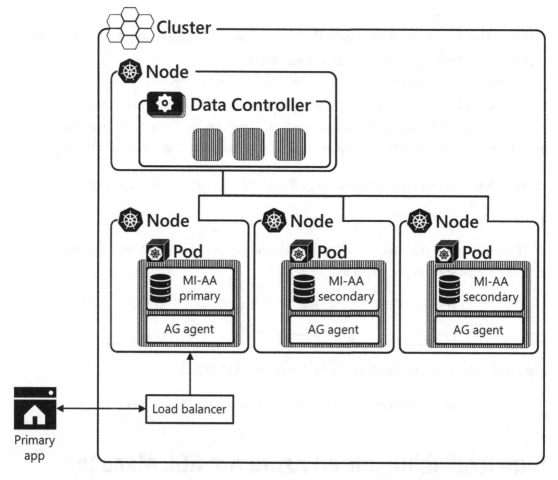

Figure 9-14. *SQL Managed Instance Always On availability group*

When deploying an Azure Arc–enabled *SQL Managed Instance Always On availability group*, it offers the following capabilities:

1. The three-replica group is managed internally, including creation of the availability group and joining replicas to the availability group created.

2. All databases are automatically added to the availability group, including all user and system databases like *master* and msdb. This capability provides a single system view across the availability group replicas.

3. An external endpoint is automatically provisioned for connecting to databases within the availability group for both read-write and read-only connections.

4. Ability to run read-only workloads by connecting to the secondary instances.

5. Automated failovers and instance redeployment in the event of pod or node failure.

6. Upgrades are managed.

Deploying a Managed Instance backed by multiple replicas is almost too easy. To deploy an Azure Arc SQL Managed Instance as an AG, all you need to do is add the *replicas* switch to your create command as shown in Listing 9-10.

Listing 9-10. azdata command to create a new SQL Managed Instance with parameters

```
azdata arc sql mi create \
      --name arc-mi-ha \
      --replicas 3
```

Once this deployment has finished, we can retrieve the primary's endpoint and run the command in Listing 9-11 against it to check the state of our availability group.

Listing 9-11. Get AG health through T-SQL

```
SELECT ag.name agname, ags.* FROM sys.dm_hadr_availability_group_states ags
INNER JOIN sys.availability_groups ag ON ag.group_id = ags.group_id
```

As you can see in Figure 9-15, everything is looking fine.

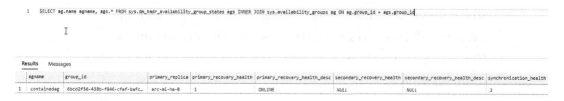

Figure 9-15. *State of AG*

Just for reference, if we run the same query against our single instance deployment, this query will come back empty (see Figure 9-16).

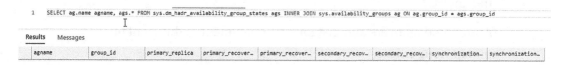

Figure 9-16. *No availability group deployed*

Also take note (Figure 9-17) that our HA instance was deployed using three pods rather than just one – you can verify that using `kubectl get pods` again.

```
arc-mi-ha-0        4/4      Running    0          4m46s
arc-mi-ha-1        4/4      Running    0          4m46s
arc-mi-ha-2        4/4      Running    0          4m46s
```

Figure 9-17. *Pods for Managed Instance AG in Azure Arc namespace*

Note   Here we see three replicas running in a StatefulSet with each pod running four containers.

Summary

In this chapter, we looked at Azure Arc–enabled Data Services and how they allow the deployment of complex solutions by adding another layer of abstraction through *azdata*. We deployed an Azure Arc–enabled Data Controller as well as an Azure Arc Managed Instance and made it highly available by deploying it as an availability group. In our next and last chapter, we will look at another SQL Server implementation running on Kubernetes: Big Data Clusters.

CHAPTER 10

Big Data Clusters

Now that we know how to deploy SQL Server on Kubernetes, let's look in our last chapter at how Microsoft designed, built, and deployed Big Data Clusters to run in Kubernetes and the challenges encountered and solutions crafted to build a complex distributed system in Kubernetes and ship it as a product. We will look at the BDC architecture and map that back to Kubernetes objects and constructs.

Introduction to Big Data Clusters

SQL Server 2019 Big Data Clusters – or just Big Data Clusters – are a new feature set within SQL Server 2019 with a broad range of functionality around data virtualization, data mart scale-out, and artificial intelligence. Despite Microsoft's "cloud-first" strategy to release new features and functionality to Azure first and eventually roll them over to the on-premises versions (if at all), they are part of the box product, so while you can obviously install them wherever you want, they are customer managed.

Big Data Clusters only run on Linux (let that sink in for a second!) and can only be deployed in a Kubernetes Cluster. While so far in this book we've showed you ways of deploying applications to Kubernetes as a modern alternative to classic deployments on Windows Servers, this is the point where you don't get a choice on how to deploy it. And since this is the second example after Arc–enabled Data Services which we've introduced in the previous chapter, this is hopefully also the point – if you haven't already – where you see how Kubernetes is the platform to deploy modern data applications and why it is so important to have that as part of your skillset going forward.

SQL Server 2019 Big Data Clusters are essentially a combination of SQL Server, Apache Spark, and the HDFS running in a Kubernetes environment. They are not a single feature but rather a feature set. Figure 10-1 categorizes the different parts of this feature set into different groups to help you better understand what is being provided. The overall idea is through virtualization and scale-out, SQL Server 2019 becomes your data hub for all your data, even if that data is not physically sitting in SQL Server.

© Anthony E. Nocentino, Ben Weissman 2021
A. E. Nocentino and B. Weissman, *SQL Server on Kubernetes*, https://doi.org/10.1007/978-1-4842-7192-6_10

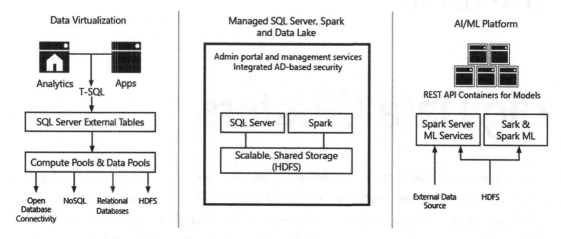

Figure 10-1. *Feature overview of SQL Server 2019 Big Data Clusters*

The major aspects of Big Data Clusters are shown from left to right. You have support for data virtualization, then a managed data platform, and finally an artificial intelligence (AI) platform.

Let's take a deeper look at them.

Data Virtualization

Data virtualization brings data into SQL Server that doesn't physically sit in SQL Server. This is implemented through PolyBase. Originally introduced in SQL Server 2016, PolyBase introduced the concept of *external tables*. While PolyBase originally only supported file-based sources, this has now been greatly enhanced to other sources like Oracle, SQL Server, Teradata, MongoDB, and countless others. This allows you to create a table dbo.Customers, for example, and query it as if it were a local table, but its data is sitting in an Azure SQL Database, for example. While this may remind you a bit of linked servers, the fact that PolyBase external tables do not require the dreaded three-dot notation (Servername.databasename.schemaname.tablename) and queries against them are multi-threaded only shows some of the advantages they offer over them.

There is no caching for external tables, so every single query against them hits the underlying source in real time, which is something you should consider – think about latency and workloads – before building your data warehouse from scratch through PolyBase ☺.

Managed Data Platform

Within the managed data platform of Big Data Clusters, you are basically offered two options: You can scale out single SQL Server tables across multiple instances of SQL Server – so instead of just spreading them over files or file groups, they are physically pushed into separate instances. Or you can store and consume file-based data like CSV or Parquet files (if you are not familiar with Parquet, think of it like a clustered column store for flat files). Those files would be exposed and accessed in SQL Server through external tables again, allowing you to potentially run a query that looks like it's consuming SQL Server data only but is in fact combining data from a CSV with a table in an Oracle instance with a big fact table that's scaled out across a few other SQL Servers with a... You get the point.

AI and Application Platform

A Big Data Cluster allows you to deploy applications that can, for example, be SSIS packages or R or Python applications. These applications can then be exposed through a REST API and accessed from within the Big Data Cluster as well as from outside. Therefore, your Big Data Cluster becomes your database, your file server, and your application server, all at the same time and all within a single deployment without worrying about connectivity between those components and pools.

BDC Architecture

Big Data Clusters can be divided into four logical layers. Consider these as a collection of various infrastructure and management parts that perform a specific function inside the cluster. Each of the areas in turn has one or more roles it performs. For instance, inside the Data layer, there are two roles: the Storage Pool and the SQL Data Pool.

Figure 10-2 shows an overview of the four logical areas and the various roles that are part of each area.

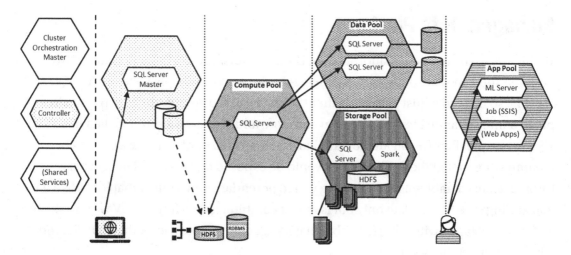

Figure 10-2. *Big Data Cluster architecture*

You can immediately infer the four logical layers: the Control layer (which internally is named the Control Plane – just like in Kubernetes itself there is another Control Plane) and the Compute, Data, and App areas.

Big Data Cluster Components

Let us take a deeper look at the components of our Big Data Cluster.

BDC Control Plane

The Control Plane – not to be confused with the Kubernetes Control Plane – of a Big Data Cluster is the centerpiece of every BDC deployment. It combines functionality like the Grafana and Kibana monitoring dashboards as well as vital functions like the control service and the configuration store. While you'll probably never interact with any of these components except for the dashboards, your BDC simply wouldn't do anything without them.

SQL Server Master Instance

You might have noticed there is an additional or almost standalone role displayed in Figure 10-2, the SQL Server Master Instance.

The SQL Server Master Instance is a SQL Server on Linux deployment and acts like an entrypoint toward your Big Data Cluster. It provides the external endpoint to connect to through Azure Data Studio or from other tools like SQL Server Management Studio.

Compute Pool

The compute pool consists of one or more SQL Server on Linux instances, allowing you to access various data sources through PolyBase in a distributed manner. For instance, a Compute Pool can access data stored inside HDFS on the Big Data Cluster itself or access data through any of the PolyBase connectors like Oracle or MongoDB.

The main advantage of a Compute Pool is that it opens up options to distribute, or scale out, queries across multiple nodes inside each Compute Pool, boosting the performance of PolyBase queries.

Every BDC deployment will have at least one SQL instance as part of the Compute Pool. You will never interact with them directly – except for debugging purposes maybe – and they will just transparently be part of your query executions across your cluster.

Storage Pool

The storage pool provides you an HDFS Cluster with Apache Spark and SQL Server endpoints. Just like with the Compute Pool, every BDC has at least one instance as part of its Storage Pool, but you can also decide for more, depending on your workloads and use cases. This means that every Big Data Cluster comes with its own HDFS and therefore is able to self-host any file-based data you may need to consume within your cluster. If you already have an HDFS store in, for example, Azure Data Lake Store (ADLS), you can also add this as a mountpoint through so-called tiering. Your ADLS would in this case just become a folder within your storage pool.

Data Pool

The data pool on the other hand provides you multiple SQL Server on Linux Pods/ instances that can – again through the concept of an external table – be used to scale out single tables across them. In theory, you could also deploy your data pool with just one single instance like all the other pools. This only makes sense in a scenario, though, where you're not going to make use of the data pool as you obviously can't scale out a table with just a single instance. You can think of a scaled-out table on the data pool like a UNION ALL – you run a single query against a table and get the result of multiple physical tables. The data pool only supports INSERT and TRUNCATE operations and is not transaction aware, so do not consider this your primary data store but rather a cache for SQL Server data.

Application Pool

The last component is the application pool. It allows you to deploy MLeap, R, Python, or SSIS solutions to it through Azure Data Studio, Visual Studio Code, or the command line using azdata. Those applications can then be consumed either interactively, through a REST API, or based on a schedule.

Kubernetes Constructs in BDC

Every BDC will be deployed to its own namespace, which is by default *mssql-cluster*, within a Kubernetes cluster. The different components within a BDC are represented by individual pods. Within the different pools, every instance of the data pool, for example, will be represented by its own pod. The output of a list of pods within a BDC, retrieved through kubectl, can be seen in Figure 10-3.

```
bdc@bdcLinux:~$ kubectl get pods -n mssql-cluster
NAME              READY   STATUS    RESTARTS   AGE
appproxy-n7vlw    2/2     Running   0          25m
compute-0-0       3/3     Running   0          25m
control-s8t9w     3/3     Running   0          30m
controldb-0       2/2     Running   0          29m
controlwd-bt5fn   1/1     Running   0          28m
data-0-0          3/3     Running   0          25m
data-0-1          3/3     Running   0          25m
gateway-0         2/2     Running   0          25m
logsdb-0          1/1     Running   0          28m
logsui-1bb4f      1/1     Running   0          28m
master-0          3/3     Running   0          25m
metricsdb-0       1/1     Running   0          28m
metricsdc-9dvcz   1/1     Running   0          28m
metricsui-2rd7j   1/1     Running   0          28m
mgmtproxy-g949x   2/2     Running   0          28m
nmnode-0-0        2/2     Running   0          25m
sparkhead-0       4/4     Running   0          25m
storage-0-0       4/4     Running   0          25m
storage-0-1       4/4     Running   0          25m
bdc@bdcLinux:~$ []
```

Figure 10-3. *Output of kubectl get pods in a BDC namespace*

In this example, we can see that this specific deployment consists of two instances each in the data and storage pools vs. one instance each in the app and compute pools and one or more pods of each of the other components like the *metricsdb, metricsdc,* and *metricsui* pods, which, for example, represent the Grafana dashboard. As you can probably tell by now, with us deploying Grafana and Kibana in Chapter 8, them being shipped with Azure Arc–enabled Data Services as showcased in Chapter 9, and them now resurfacing yet again, they have become the de facto standard for monitoring and log management in the SQL Server on Kubernetes world.

The BDC's endpoints are exposed in Kubernetes through services. Depending on the platform, those will either be of type NodePort or *LoadBalancer*, as we can see in our example in Figure 10-4.

```
bdc@bdcLinux:~$ kubectl get services -n mssql-cluster | grep NodePort
appproxy-svc-external       NodePort    10.98.54.124      <none>        8080:30778/TCP

controller-svc-external     NodePort    10.104.130.185    <none>        8443:30080/TCP

gateway-svc-external        NodePort    10.106.64.232     <none>        8443:30443/TCP

master-svc-external         NodePort    10.110.148.127    <none>        1433:31433/TCP

mgmtproxy-svc-external      NodePort    10.106.87.204     <none>        8443:30777/TCP

bdc@bdcLinux:~$ []
```

Figure 10-4. *Output of kubectl get services | grep NodePort in a BDC namespace*

In addition to these services, it also exposes a number of *ClusterIP* services to allow the services to communicate with each other.

It also creates numerous different sets – DaemonSets, ReplicaSets, and StatefulSets. If we list them using kubectl get all -n mssql-cluster, they all show up in the lower part of the output (Figure 10-5).

```
NAME                          DESIRED    CURRENT    READY    UP-TO-DATE    AVAILABLE    NODE SELECTOR    AGE
daemonset.apps/metricsdc      1          1          1        1             1            <none>           28m

NAME                          DESIRED    CURRENT    READY    AGE
replicaset.apps/appproxy      1          1          1        25m
replicaset.apps/control       1          1          1        29m
replicaset.apps/controlwd     1          1          1        28m
replicaset.apps/logsui        1          1          1        28m
replicaset.apps/metricsui     1          1          1        28m
replicaset.apps/mgmtproxy     1          1          1        28m

NAME                          READY      AGE
statefulset.apps/compute-0    1/1        25m
statefulset.apps/controldb    1/1        29m
statefulset.apps/data-0       2/2        25m
statefulset.apps/gateway      1/1        25m
statefulset.apps/logsdb       1/1        28m
statefulset.apps/master       0/1        25m
statefulset.apps/metricsdb    1/1        28m
statefulset.apps/nmnode-0     1/1        25m
statefulset.apps/sparkhead    1/1        24m
statefulset.apps/storage-0    2/2        24m
```

Figure 10-5. *Kubernetes sets in a Big Data Cluster*

Storage in a BDC is addressed through storage classes and dynamic provisioning within these. As you can see in Figure 10-6, Big Data Clusters will create dynamic persistent volume claims (and the underlying volumes) as needed.

```
NAME                 STATUS    VOLUME                 CAPACITY    ACCESS MODES    STORAGECLASS     AGE
data-compute-0-0     Bound     local-pv-5c9fe530      193Gi       RWO             local-storage    11m
data-controldb       Bound     local-pv-98a58ffa      193Gi       RWO             local-storage    15m
data-controller      Bound     local-pv-4f90eeca      193Gi       RWO             local-storage    15m
data-data-0-0        Bound     local-pv-fe098a9e      193Gi       RWO             local-storage    11m
data-data-0-1        Bound     local-pv-44298ade      193Gi       RWO             local-storage    11m
data-gateway-0       Bound     local-pv-3bf78f06      193Gi       RWO             local-storage    10m
data-logsdb-0        Bound     local-pv-d229ecd       193Gi       RWO             local-storage    13m
data-master-0        Bound     local-pv-72eabff       193Gi       RWO             local-storage    11m
data-metricsdb-0     Bound     local-pv-f3901f8f      193Gi       RWO             local-storage    13m
data-nmnode-0-0      Bound     local-pv-f598d6d4      193Gi       RWO             local-storage    11m
data-sparkhead-0     Bound     local-pv-46d39f21      193Gi       RWO             local-storage    10m
data-storage-0-0     Bound     local-pv-7b4fd85c      193Gi       RWO             local-storage    10m
data-storage-0-1     Bound     local-pv-229a0a94      193Gi       RWO             local-storage    10m
logs-compute-0-0     Bound     local-pv-8a81b10c      193Gi       RWO             local-storage    11m
logs-controldb       Bound     local-pv-4e704dd9      193Gi       RWO             local-storage    15m
logs-controller      Bound     local-pv-e18e0041      193Gi       RWO             local-storage    15m
logs-data-0-0        Bound     local-pv-8fdda98e      193Gi       RWO             local-storage    11m
logs-data-0-1        Bound     local-pv-258afa3b      193Gi       RWO             local-storage    11m
logs-gateway-0       Bound     local-pv-12911449      193Gi       RWO             local-storage    10m
logs-logsdb-0        Bound     local-pv-bc7fbf1b      193Gi       RWO             local-storage    13m
logs-master-0        Bound     local-pv-e1b129cb      193Gi       RWO             local-storage    11m
logs-metricsdb-0     Bound     local-pv-9269a205      193Gi       RWO             local-storage    13m
logs-nmnode-0-0      Bound     local-pv-bdc3d765      193Gi       RWO             local-storage    11m
logs-sparkhead-0     Bound     local-pv-93711479      193Gi       RWO             local-storage    10m
logs-storage-0-0     Bound     local-pv-e787c46f      193Gi       RWO             local-storage    10m
logs-storage-0-1     Bound     local-pv-fff11b99      193Gi       RWO             local-storage    10m
```

Figure 10-6. *PVCs in a Big Data Cluster*

As you can see, a Big Data Cluster is really bringing everything together that we've touched so far from Kubernetes objects over monitoring to, of course, SQL Server.

Deployment

Just like Azure Arc–enabled Data Services, Big Data Clusters are being deployed through azdata, and the process can – again – be run from the command line or from Azure Data Studio, which will create a notebook that would then run azdata in the background.

Deploying a BDC requires a working Kubernetes cluster in place, which can be running on kubeadm, AKS, EKS, or OpenShift.

To deploy your BDC, you will change your Kubernetes context to the desired target cluster and create a configuration using the code in Listing 10-1.

Listing 10-1. Create a BDC configuration

```
azdata bdc config init [--path] [--source -s]
```

Path is just the folder name where the configuration files for your BDC (*bdc.json* and *control.json*) will be created at by the command in Listing 10-1. The *src* is one of the existing base templates to start with like *aks-dev-test* or *kubeadm-prod*.

A full command to create a Big Data Cluster configuration in a subfolder called *myBDC* that is supposed to be deployed on AKS using a typical development/test environment would be, for example, as shown in Listing 10-2.

Listing 10-2. Create a BDC configuration

```
azdata bdc config init --path myBDC --source aks-dev-test
```

Those files will be used to configure everything around your deployment from a potential integration of your Big Data Cluster into your Active Directory for AD authentication over the number of replicas within each pool to the memory and storage requirements. An example of one of these two files, bdc.json, can be seen in Listing 10-3.

Listing 10-3. Sample bdc.json

```
{
    "apiVersion": "v1",
    "metadata": {
        "kind": "BigDataCluster",
        "name": "mssql-cluster"
    },
    "spec": {
        "resources": {
            "nmnode-0": {
                "spec": {
                    "replicas": 2
                }
            },
            "sparkhead": {
                "spec": {
                    "replicas": 2
                }
            },
            "zookeeper": {
                "spec": {
                    "replicas": 3
                }
            },
            "gateway": {
                "spec": {
                    "replicas": 1,
                    "endpoints": [
                        {
                            "name": "Knox",
                            "dnsName": "",
                            "serviceType": "NodePort",
                            "port": 30443
                        }
                    ]
```

```
        }
    },
    "appproxy": {
        "spec": {
            "replicas": 1,
            "endpoints": [
                {
                    "name": "AppServiceProxy",
                    "dnsName": "",
                    "serviceType": "NodePort",
                    "port": 30778
                }
            ]
        }
    },
    "master": {
        "metadata": {
            "kind": "Pool",
            "name": "default"
        },
        "spec": {
            "type": "Master",
            "replicas": 3,
            "endpoints": [
                {
                    "name": "Master",
                    "dnsName": "",
                    "serviceType": "NodePort",
                    "port": 31433
                },
                {
                    "name": "MasterSecondary",
                    "dnsName": "",
                    "serviceType": "NodePort",
                    "port": 31436
```

```
                }
            ],
            "settings": {
                "sql": {
                    "hadr.enabled": "true"
                }
            }
        }
    },
    "compute-0": {
        "metadata": {
            "kind": "Pool",
            "name": "default"
        },
        "spec": {
            "type": "Compute",
            "replicas": 1
        }
    },
    "data-0": {
        "metadata": {
            "kind": "Pool",
            "name": "default"
        },
        "spec": {
            "type": "Data",
            "replicas": 2
        }
    },
    "storage-0": {
        "metadata": {
            "kind": "Pool",
            "name": "default"
        },
        "spec": {
```

```
            "type": "Storage",
            "replicas": 3,
            "settings": {
                "spark": {
                    "includeSpark": "true"
                }
            }
        }
    }
},
"services": {
    "sql": {
        "resources": [
            "master",
            "compute-0",
            "data-0",
            "storage-0"
        ]
    },
    "hdfs": {
        "resources": [
            "nmnode-0",
            "zookeeper",
            "storage-0",
            "sparkhead"
        ],
        "settings": {
            "hdfs-site.dfs.replication": "3"
        }
    },
    "spark": {
        "resources": [
            "sparkhead",
            "storage-0"
        ],
```

```
            "settings": {
                "spark-defaults-conf.spark.driver.memory": "2g",
                "spark-defaults-conf.spark.driver.cores": "1",
                "spark-defaults-conf.spark.executor.instances": "3",
                "spark-defaults-conf.spark.executor.memory": "1536m",
                "spark-defaults-conf.spark.executor.cores": "1",
                "yarn-site.yarn.nodemanager.resource.memory-mb":
                "18432",
                "yarn-site.yarn.nodemanager.resource.cpu-vcores": "6",
                "yarn-site.yarn.scheduler.maximum-allocation-mb": "18432",
                "yarn-site.yarn.scheduler.maximum-allocation-vcores": "6",
                "yarn-site.yarn.scheduler.capacity.maximum-am-resource-
                percent": "0.3"
            }
        }
      }
    }
}
```

Once you've edited/created your configuration file, you can run the azdata as shown in Listing 10-4 to create your cluster.

Listing 10-4. Create cluster using azdata

```
azdata bdc create -c < yourPath> --accept-eula yes
```

Azdata will prompt you for a username and password unless you've provided these through environment variables before. Depending on the extent of your deployment and the performance of your Kubernetes cluster, this may take anywhere from minutes to hours.

You can follow the progress and see when it completes as can be seen in Figure 10-7.

```
bdc@bdcLinux:~$ azdata bdc create -c kubeadm-custom
The privacy statement can be viewed at:
https://go.microsoft.com/fwlink/?LinkId=853010

The license terms for SQL Server Big Data Cluster can be viewed at:
Enterprise: https://go.microsoft.com/fwlink/?linkid=2104292
Standard: https://go.microsoft.com/fwlink/?linkid=2104294
Developer: https://go.microsoft.com/fwlink/?linkid=2104079

Do you accept the license terms? (y/n): y

Cluster deployment documentation can be viewed at:
https://aka.ms/bdc-deploy

Azdata username:bdc
Azdata password:
Confirm Azdata password:

NOTE: Cluster creation can take a significant amount of time depending on
configuration, network speed, and the number of nodes in the cluster.

Starting cluster deployment.
Waiting for cluster controller to start.
Waiting for cluster controller to start.
Cluster controller endpoint is available at 192.168.1.4:30080.
Cluster control plane is ready.
Data pool is ready.
Storage pool is ready.
Master pool is ready.
Compute pool is ready.
Cluster 'mssql-cluster' deployed successfully.
bdc@bdcLinux:~$ []
```

Figure 10-7. *Output of azdata bdc create*

The duration taken for the deployment will also depend on whether the images had already been pre-pulled as these alone require more than 30GB to download.

Monitoring and Management

A BDC can be monitored directly from within Azure Data Studio as well as through the Grafana and Kibana dashboards, which we've already encountered in the previous chapters as you can see in Figure 10-8. Also note how you can change the general behavior (like dark mode vs. light mode) of the portal and how this dashboard is again slightly different from the ones we've used in the previous chapters.

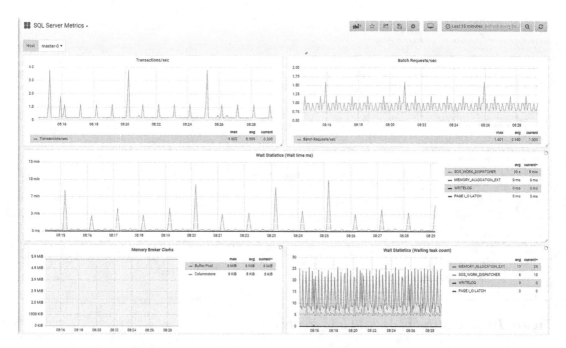

Figure 10-8. Grafana Portal – SQL Server Metrics

Azure Data Studio provides you an overview of a cluster's endpoints as well as a rough status about its health as shown in Figure 10-9.

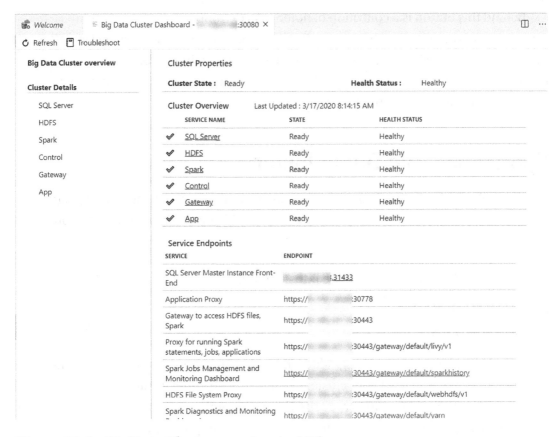

Figure 10-9. *Big Data Cluster overview in ADS*

In addition to that, as you can see in Figure 10-10, it also has a troubleshooting toolset for your BDC.

Figure 10-10. *Link to troubleshooting in ADS*

Behind this button is a collection of notebooks to troubleshoot every single component of your cluster. The first notebook to open is "TSG100 – The Big Data Cluster troubleshooter," which will guide you through a full debugging of your Big Data Cluster. If you have already narrowed down which service is causing issues, you can also navigate directly to the analyzer notebook for that specific component.

Upgrading a Big Data Cluster

Upgrades of a BDC happen through azdata, so first make sure that you have the latest version of azdata installed. To do so, run the code in Listing 10-5 just like when you first installed azdata.

Listing 10-5. Update azdata to the latest version

```
curl -o azdata.msi https://aka.ms/azdata-msi
msiexec azdata.msi
```

Now you can use *azdata* to upgrade your cluster. The command for this is *azdata bdc upgrade,* followed by at least your cluster's name and the target version.

To upgrade to Big Data Clusters 2019 CU9, for example, you would use the command shown in Listing 10-6. This will update all your BDC's components.

Listing 10-6. Upgrade your BDC to CU9 using azdata

```
azdata bdc upgrade --name mybdc --tag 2019-CU9-ubuntu-16.04
```

This will take some time as all the individual images will need to be pulled first followed by an upgrade of every single component in your cluster. Just like during the installation process, the upgrade process will give you a continuous status update on which component it is currently working at up to the point where the upgrade process is complete.

At this point, there is no way to change the size of a Big Data Cluster post deployment, so azdata can upgrade an existing cluster to another version, but you could not change the number of instances in a pool, for example. This would require a new deployment.

If you want to learn more about Big Data Clusters including details on how to deploy them, we recommend the Apress book *SQL Server Big Data Clusters: Data Virtualization, Data Lake, and AI Platform.*

Summary

In this final chapter, we explored how Kubernetes can be used to deploy very complex and heterogeneous applications like Big Data Clusters in a simple and automated way. This also concludes this book. We hope this helped you to gain a deeper understanding about Kubernetes and how it can help you to deploy modern data applications!

Index

G, H

I, J

K, L

Printed in the United States
by Baker & Taylor Publisher Services